P9-CQQ-304

MARRIED MY MOM, BIRTHED A DOG

How to be Resilient When Life Sucks

MARRIED MY MOM, BIRTHED A DOG

How to be Resilient When Life Sucks

ELEVATE PRESS

A DIVISION OF ELEVATE SEMINARS AND STRATEGIC DEVELOPMENT INC.

Disclaimer: *This book is about my experiences overcoming physical and emotional challenges. While others have found these approaches helpful, my ideas are not a substitute for professional assistance. Please seek immediate treatment from qualified health care professionals should you be experiencing severe trauma, mental health issues or any other adversity that requires specialized insights, as I am not a doctor.*

Married My Mom, Birthed A Dog

Copyright © 2017 by Allison Graham

www.ElevateBiz.com

2018 Elevate Press Edition

All rights reserved. The scanning, uploading, and electronic sharing of any part of this book without the permission of the author constitutes unlawful piracy and theft of the author's intellectual property. If you would like to use material from the book (other than for review purposes), prior written permission must be obtained by contacting the author.

ISBN (e-book): 978-0-9810623-4-1
ISBN (paperback): 978-0-9810623-3-4
ISBN (hardcover): 978-0-9810623-2-7

*To you, the reader: thank you for letting me share.
I hope my story, with all its mistakes and triumphs,
will help you through yours.*

*To Mom and Winston C: thank you for being my
lifelines when I was sinking in quicksand. I love you.*

To my family and friends: XOXO

*To the incredible healthcare professionals who helped
me on my journey: thank you for your expertise,
kindness and commitment to good patient care.*

Table of Contents

Welcome

I IMAGINE YOU AND ME sitting together in big comfy chairs, with our favorite drink in hand, chatting about what I've written, swapping stories and laughing until our bellies hurt. Sometimes humor is the best medicine.

We wouldn't rehash the past like it's a caged identity, but more like a movie with twists and turns in its plot and we're in charge of crafting the ending.

We'd swap lessons learned and offer each other support without judgment or comparison. By the end of our visit we would feel refreshed, empowered and ready to embrace all the world offers.

If you're up for that, then welcome to my book.

As you read this introduction, I must admit, I'm the reader who skips ahead to chapter one to plunge right into the good stuff. That makes writing this section a bit challenging.

My Mom is the opposite of me. She loves to dive into details usually provided in introductions and prologues, so she knows what to expect before reading a book. If you're like my mom, you may be disappointed to get just a hint of my background now, but I'm confident you'll get more than enough details as you continue. What I went through is the backdrop for all the lessons unveiled in the chapters that follow.

Even though I'm sharing my saga, these pages are not just about my story; they're about reflecting your story in mine. I know you have a story, and probably more than one, because dealing with problems is one of humanity's universal truths.

This is a hybrid of a storybook and a traditional self-help book, so you'll notice I routinely switch between sharing my experiences and offering tools to help you move ahead quickly when life just sucks.

My hope is that you'll feel less alone during tough times, less judgmental in moments of self-doubt, and more confident when dealing with life's hiccups. Ideally, you'll find the blessings hidden within your trials and learn from my mistakes, so that you can fast-track your journey to Resiliency Ninja.

You'll learn how to master my formula by the end of this book. You will find even more resources such as videos and blog posts at www.r-Ninja.com. Also, don't forget to subscribe to my Resiliency Ninja podcast.

So why did I write this book? After all, we all have stories of struggle, but that doesn't mean everyone wants to reveal what's behind their curtain. I recognize that being publicly vulnerable carries significant risk, but even so, after surviving my decade of hell I feel compelled to help you find joy amidst your worst challenges.

The last decade has given me a lot of reasons to practice my skills as a Resiliency Ninja. I'm a business owner who regularly attends community events and does some media work. Behind my polished exterior, I deal with chronic neuropathic pain from a botched surgery. I've also experienced hard knocks such as grief, financial challenges, fluke injuries, loss of friendships – and self-doubt that compounded the impact of every setback. Despite the odds, I had some amazing adventures, grew a successful career and found peace along my journey. I want that for you, too.

As I share my string of unfortunate events and the tools I used to succeed, I recognize that my ways are not the only ways that work. Please consider my advice and mull it around to create the best approach for your needs. There are no "one-size fits-all" solutions in life.

When I was in the thick of my physical and emotional pain, and felt the most lost both personally and professionally, I needed help. Unfortunately, I couldn't find a book or a coaching program that addressed all the related aspects of my adversity. I hope this book, my podcast and my Resiliency Ninja coaching programs, will give you the insights that I so desperately was looking for early in my decade of hell.

The joke that became my book title, *Married My Mom, Birthed A Dog*, started in 2010. I'll share more about what that means as we go, but for now I'll just say that I'm happy to honor my mom for standing by my side through turbulent times.

I'm also excited to showcase my dog Winston C. who has no idea what's happening as you may have noticed from his facial expression on the cover. He just knows I'm spending a lot of hours in front of my laptop. As any four-legged loyal companion would do, he just goes with the flow and offers love.

Obviously, I did not literally marry my mom or birth a dog: it's just that on many days it's felt like I have.

We all have our own path. This just happens to be mine...

1

Whack-a-Mole

DESPITE ALL THE BLESSINGS OF being alive, there are times when life just sucks. Life is a master at beating us up in gut-wrenching ways that are out of our control.

Unfortunately, as adults we're not afforded the luxury of wallowing in our problems, even when we want to hide under our blankets, scream in defeat and wait for the universe to make everything peachy-keen again. (I've tried that, it doesn't work.)

Instead, we must strike our best superhero pose in front of the proverbial fan as it blows high-velocity shit in our face – and we have to do so with a big smile because, heaven forbid, if we slip and fail publicly, what would "they" think?

In the end, it does not matter what everyone else thinks, it matters what *you* think. The uninvited peanut gallery that spews judgment is not the benchmark by which to measure success, especially when even the slightest negative views are magnified by the unforgiving voice inside your head.

Do you remember the game Whack-a-Mole? When I was young I would play it at summer fairs. Using that big foam hammer to whack those plastic moles into their holes when they popped was lots of fun. I was pretty good at hitting the first few, but as the moles started appearing and disappearing more quickly, it proved to be too much for my hammering skills. Another mole appeared, faster, faster and faster and sooner, rather than later, I'd lose.

Little did I know that game would become a metaphor for my future.

Have you ever felt like life is an unending game of full-sized Whack-a-Mole, swatting down one problem just in time for another to erupt?

On Christmas Eve 2008, I had my fourth surgery to fix the ramifications from an earlier botched surgery that caused unrelenting neuropathic pain and other complications. Weeks later there was a string of sudden deaths of people close to me. I was heartbroken. Shaken to my core. Intellectually I knew there was light at the end of the tunnel, but there were many dark days when I just couldn't see its glow or feel its warmth.

Days after attending my fifth funeral in three months I had a lunch meeting with two bigwigs from an investment firm. We met to discuss how I could help their advisors get more sales and network more effectively – trust me, there is irony in that statement.

Physically I was in excruciating pain and emotionally I was beyond spent. It was not the first time I had forced myself to act professionally while ignoring my personal nightmares, but this time was different. The moles were erupting, and they were winning. My heart was heavy, and my body was weak. The prospective clients talked and all I heard was blah, blah, blah. With each passing minute, I daydreamed of my couch, comfy clothes and a full DVR of TV shows just waiting to help me go numb.

It was the worst lunch meeting conversation I've ever had and it was my fault. Just painful. It's the kind of teeth-pulling, one-word answers, nothing-is-flowing discussion that makes people loathe getting-to-know-you-business meetings. At one point they ignored me and started talking with each other. That's never a good sign when you're selling training programs on how to connect with prospects.

To encourage some interesting comments from my side of the table one prospect asked, "What hobbies fill your spare time?" For a split-second, I recognized this was my chance to turn around this lack-luster impression I was making and save the deal. I could say anything interesting. I love downhill skiing, sailing, hiking, volunteering for charities, politics, you name it. I had many good answers.

What did I say?

"I like to watch TV."

Silence.

And now my internal dialogue really heated up, "*WTF did you just say? Did you just tell these prospects, senior execs, that your big hobby is watching television? That's not even a hobby. What is wrong with you?*"

They graciously inquired about my favorite shows, and the conversation became more engaging. Soon after, I resumed my favorite position on my couch.

The reason I remember that lunch so vividly is because it was a turning point. The collision between my personal and professional lives hit me like a ton of bricks.

Sure, throwing TV-watching into the hobby bucket is ill-advised when trying to impress high-powered executives, but that's not what bothered me the most. It was how disappointed I was that I had been so completely unengaged while sitting with two other human beings. I was embarrassed that I was letting my own problems consume me and prevent me from showing up as the best version of myself. They deserved better.

That failed meeting prevented me from adding two influencers to my network, serving a hundred professionals and landing a contract I desperately needed.

I realized this was a time for a serious shift. The next day I turned my focus to becoming a Resiliency Ninja. It was my choice to make: either be a victim of my circumstances or rise from my hell even stronger.

If you're going through bad times right now, you have the same choice.

Until that lunch I had taken for granted that, with a moment's notice, I could switch gears from despair to power-player mode in business. Apparently, that wasn't a sustainable approach.

Just like when you play Whack-a-Mole, you never know what issue is going to pop up anytime to knock you off your best game. At some point, something will happen in your personal life that makes showing up professionally difficult and vice versa. In a perfect world, personal and professional issues would never collide; the fan would blow work issues between 9 A.M. and 5 P.M. and personal problems after hours. Unfortunately, the fan blows directly at you, indiscriminately, 24/7. When work suffers, stress increases and strains collect on the home front. A difficult home life spills into your work. There it goes; around and around like a vicious cycle. That's why you need to be able to deal with roadblocks as they appear, rather than letting them derail your dreams.

At the time of that failed lunch meeting, Mom was not yet living with me and I had not yet found my dog, Winston C.

Before they became an active part of my day-to-day, I was going through physical pain, grief and depression all on my own. Despite having a strong professional network, I was feeling exceptionally isolated. If you've ever felt the depths of loneliness when you're surrounded by a crowd, you'll relate to the overwhelming sadness that can consume your very being.

Among the first moles I couldn't whack down was the loss of my Dad. He was my sounding board and best friend for the first 30 years of my life. His death left a gaping hole in my soul that I tried to stuff full by being busy-busy. To give you a sense of the unrealistic pace I was keeping, the year after he died I went to 241 events. That's a lot of schmoozing. If my career wasn't busy enough, I filled my time with retail therapy shopping for stuff I did not need or by doing low-value, mind-numbing tasks.

Dad's mom, my Grandma Graham, passed away suddenly on his birthday 10 months later that same year. She mentioned Robbie's birthday, then asked her caretaker for a glass of water and a Tylenol. By the time the nurse returned, Grandma was gone. I think she just couldn't handle the devastation from losing two of her sons, as my uncle had died from cancer a couple years earlier.

The proverbial fan didn't slow down after the first few blows. It just kept increasing speed.

The nastiest baseline issue for me has been the unrelenting, chronic neuropathic pain I mentioned earlier. It was caused in 2007 by a simple surgery that went terribly wrong. There were subsequent surgeries to attempt to fix the first, followed by eight random physical injuries requiring hospital visits, treatments and additional surgeries in a span of a few years, a cluster of deaths of people close to me in a matter of months and all the emotional, mental and financial turmoil that you'd expect from such hardships.

Add in some bad choices with men, some crummy business coaches, all the regular stress of running a business and maintaining a professional image; top it all with a dollop of self-judgment and a tendency for self-sabotage, and, well…I'm writing this book.

Instinctively, I was resourceful and independent probably because I had no choice but to be just that. There was no husband to help me pay my bills and I was, and still am, my own boss.

Doctors suggested I go on government disability, take strong pain pills for the rest of my life and learn to "pace" myself. None of those options interested me. They felt like cop-outs.

Having just celebrated over 10 years in business, a milestone that statistically only four percent of small business owners reach, it's surreal to look back and realize all the obstacles I had to overcome on my journey.

Throughout all of it, if you asked my clients – and some of them are heavy-hitting corporations and institutions – they would have no idea I was battling neuropathic pain, going through the grieving process, or worrying about the significant debt I created after the surgeries and some bad business decisions.

An outsider just saw the happy social media photos, the professional speaker on stage and my contributions in the media. They assumed everything was normal while I was playing real-life Whack-a-Mole.

As I write this I realize how far I've come because I've reset the emotions that kept me anchored in anguish. Piecing together the perspectives and techniques that allowed me to find peace in my nightmare decade has filled me with gratitude. Years ago, I would not have been able to say that. So many other emotions—resentment, anger, dissatisfaction and embarrassment—consumed my mind and heart. Thankfully I've worked through those negative emotions, which is why I can share these ideas with you from a place of hope.

Successfully overcoming obstacles brings a deep-rooted confidence that enables greater success and a more authentic, joyful existence.

My hard times inspired a new way of life. I was forced to take back control of my schedule, shape a highly profitable business and stop owning 'busy' as a badge of honor. I'm even better equipped to manage my nerve pain without having to take heavy medications as I did before.

Best of all, it was because of the pain that Mom moved to my city to live with me. Out of necessity she became my caregiver, my chauffeur for five years and surprisingly, much like a life partner. The situation also led to some frustrations, as you might imagine, when two previously independent adults combine their lives. It's not unlike the adjustments people make when they combine homes with a significant other.

Even better than the best of all (if that's possible) was finding my dog Winston C. (FYI, the "C" stands for Cutest Dog Ever, not Churchill, like so many people expect.) He has been a constant source of love and joy in my life, no matter the day's challenges.

It takes a rare combination of finessing several skills to become a master Resiliency Ninja. You'll need to learn to honor yourself, accept life's ups and downs, keep your thinking in check, find the silver linings in bad situations and be exceptionally resourceful as you strive to reach your goals. Mastering these elements means you can still succeed even when your heart is breaking, your body is saying no, and the odds are stacked against you. It also means you'll be comfortable taking time to heal without guilt.

Adversity is a fact of life, but even the most difficult circumstances don't have to keep you down. Success is achieved when you embrace life's challenges—whatever they may be. You can become a master at bouncing forward. Notice I didn't say bouncing back, because to bounce back would insinuate that it is possible to go back to the way things were before adversity struck and that's impossible. Even so, hope is not lost. I'll show you how to become a Resiliency Ninja, as I map the tools and thinking tactics I used to keep myself moving ahead when life sucked. As you read through my story, I hope you will find it easier to cope and to thrive in the midst of yours.

I know you are playing your own version of Whack-a-Mole that is invisible to outsiders. Ultimately, you need to find your own rhythm and the best way to whack down the next issue and the next, like a ninja. Otherwise the bad stuff can consume you, the buzzer will sound, and you'll lose.

It's your choice to decide if you will win or lose in the face of adversity. Unfortunately for many, when adversity shows up they suck it in as if its Vick's VapoRub® and hold their breath forever. They drop their personal power and believe there is no solution.

There is always a solution.

2

Vertical Equals Superstar Status

WHEN ONE OF MY DOCTORS pointed out my knack for bouncing back from hard-knocks time and time again, I was kind of surprised. Who, me? Resilient? Obviously, this doc didn't realize I felt like I was drowning in an ocean of tears. She was definitely unaware of the number of days I clung to my couch for a Netflix marathon as if it was the last life raft on the Titanic.

After a longer conversation on the topic I realized that being resilient doesn't mean that you always feel positive, or that every day is a power day. In fact, many days are not.

Most "resilience" stories are about superstars: the climbers of Mount Everest, the Olympic athletes who overcame every obstacle to claim the podium or the millionaire who went bankrupt and returned even stronger and wealthier.

Stories like these fill me with admiration. They inspire almost anyone to be better, think bigger and eliminate excuses. Often, however, it seemed such a huge leap from where I was to where these incredible humans have landed. I found it difficult to relate to their stories. On many days through this journey, my proverbial mountain was just getting out of bed to work. My version of climbing Everest was simply achieving vertical, so the idea of aiming for real summits was nowhere in my mind.

That's why this book is for the rest of us: the superstars of daily life.

The ones who get to the end of a day and know we did our best, even if no one else recognizes how much we had to overcome to do so. It's for those of us who are struggling silently, frustrated with current circumstances and uncertain of what direction to go next, as we scream into the ether, "Is *this* really my life?"

There are some days when you are celebrating a huge win and other days when achieving vertical equals superstar status. In other words, you don't need to climb Mount Everest with no hands, no feet, naked and backwards, uphill both ways to be validated as a person who has mastered resiliency and can overcome life's challenges with grace. It's all relative.

Aiming for a huge, life-altering goal may not be in your cards right now and that's okay. Focus specifically on the next steps that will get you closer to what you ultimately want to achieve.

The ideal is to take pride in what you've accomplished each day by pushing yourself even a hint farther than defeat thinks you can.

None of this means you can use tough times as an excuse to aim for mediocrity. Performing below your potential adds an extra level of frustration and despair I hope you never feel.

So how do you make strides towards your overarching objectives when everything seems to be falling apart around you?

Simply telling you to do "X", when the fan blows "Y" would be doing you a disservice. Your tactical solutions will always vary based on your circumstances and personality. Determining how to work around life's challenges is easy compared to being prepared and motivated physically, mentally and emotionally to take the right actions, time and time again, in the face of defeat.

Basically, you need to become a Resiliency Ninja.

Just like the stealthy, powerful ninja warriors in Hollywood movies, you may often find yourself engaged in a fight for your life. You may have to enter combat in secret, from the darkness of the shadows where no one else, especially your coworkers or clients, can see your struggles. Ninjas must master technical and tactical skills and they must learn to control their emotional, physical and mental well-being to fight with a sense of calmness and confidence. Whether one enemy comes at them or 100, the ninjas keep fighting, one challenger at a time, until the threat is neutralized. Always keenly aware of their surroundings, their shortcomings and their strengths, ninjas seem to emerge victorious from the worst, most terrifying scenarios.

It is through this Hollywood interpretation of a ninja that I've created my formula for being a Resiliency Ninja. What it takes to achieve superstardom—or sometimes just get vertical—is found in this formula:

Resiliency Ninja =
Self-Awareness + Strength (Heart + Mental + Physical) +
Resourcefulness.

I'll explain the formula backwards from its end to its beginning.

Resourcefulness:

What sets ninjas apart from their foes is resourcefulness. They know the tools, techniques and tactics of success that others never grasp. When the struggle is close, switching tactics and improvising new solutions usually makes the difference between winning or waving the white flag of surrender.

When it comes to being a Resiliency Ninja, resources will be all around you. It's up to you to notice them. There are people who will support you and there will be insights you garner from exercises such as those found throughout this book.

However, just being resourceful is not enough.

Physical Strength:

You will also need to develop your physical strength by learning how to tap into your body's power to carry you over rocky terrain. When adversity strikes, the first thing that often goes is focus on physical health. Taking small actions to nurture your body and ensure your surroundings are safe and supportive will help as you become a Resiliency Ninja.

Mental Strength:

You also need to sharpen your mental strength, which helps you align your thoughts to serve your best self. Many of the hardest knocks in life come from within.

Heart Strength:

The difference between giving up and rising as the victor is often hidden in your strength of heart: your ability to remain strong emotionally while embracing the heartbreaking realities around you.

Self-Awareness:

Mastering all the above skills requires concentration and will. You must become exceptionally self-aware of the challenges you're facing, discover what you need to get through them and recognize your patterns that tend to either support or destroy you.

When you combine these cornerstones of resiliency you have my formula for becoming a Resiliency Ninja:

Self-Awareness +

Strength (Heart + Mental + Physical) +

Resourcefulness = Resiliency Ninja

As you continue in this book, each chapter will address one or more elements of the formula. Key takeaways and coaching questions will be summarized at the end of each chapter. Additional resources can be found at www.R-Ninja.com. Download them today, you'll be happy you did!

If I need a boost during tough times or I'm not showing up as my best self, I look to this formula to see which areas need extra focus and TLC.

A simple way to illustrate this point is by diving into a common obstacle for many – writers' block.

I once heard bestselling author Seth Godin speak at a conference where he described the challenge of writers' block as "romanticized fiction." He explained that the tools of writing, basically just thinking and typing on a computer, or by writing in longhand, are not that difficult. I agree, especially for experienced writers.

As Seth, one of the great keynote speakers of our time gave his opinion on writers' block my Resiliency Ninja formula sharpened. It became crystal clear to me.

I've spent 15 years writing and sharing my thoughts, but that doesn't mean that every time I open my laptop the words are going to flow.

Seth explained every writer knows that the best way to overcome writers' block is to start writing. Even if it's bad prose, writers know they can always edit later. Words on a screen are fixable, but unwritten words floating in the mind can cause frustration. So why isn't knowing how to write enough?

Knowing how to write speaks to the technique and the facts, not to the emotional tug that can leave someone staring at a blank screen. What stops a writer from starting is a mental and heart-felt issue, not a resource issue.

The hardest part of creating prose is getting in the mood to write and believing that the words written will have value. It's important to become aware of destructive patterns and damaging thinking that prevent words from finding the page.

People often ask me how to write a book and so I tell them the how.

Thinking, writing and editing are three separate steps. I'll share a deeper explanation of how to approach each step, but that doesn't mean they are going to write a book; most of the time they don't. A more helpful conversation would address the emotional and mental blocks that have prevented them from writing their own book so far. Becoming self-aware and understanding their internal resistance will get them writing much faster than discussing what type of software to use.

Being resilient when life tries to drag you down is much the same thing. It's the *real* struggle no one else sees. When life is easy, of course you can smile and get stuff done, but putting a smile on your face when you're playing extreme Whack-a-Mole requires more physical, emotional and mental strength than technicalities alone can motivate. Anyone can tell you how to make a smile: curl the sides of your mouth in an upward direction. But when you're crumbling on the inside the mechanics don't matter. If you want to smile authentically, you must step back, reframe the situation and find joy in the moment.

That's why most of the stories I share include aspects that challenge how you think, feel and react to adversity. Sure, I'll show you my framework for finding the best ways to power through difficulties by being extra resourceful. Unfortunately, without the self-awareness plus the physical, mental and heart strength to inspire you to approach your problems in the right way, you will stay stuck and your adversities will dictate your outcome. If, however, you are armed with the proper insight, you'll be able to achieve the results you want no matter what flies your way.

That's what it means to be a Resiliency Ninja.

3

Top-It, Diminish-It

RECENTLY, I THREW OUT MY neck and ribcage during a night terror. I know, odd.

I spent that weekend just taking it easy. I accepted the pain and within a few days I was back to a new functioning 'normal' with a neck that wouldn't move very well. It still hurt, but I figured it would fix itself naturally.

Finally, I went to see a chiropractor. He explained that I had the equivalent of a case of whiplash caused by a 30-mile-an-hour car accident. Two appointments into treatment and I was starting to feel better.

On my way to my third chiropractor's appointment, I was on the phone with a master Top-It player. You know the type; it's the person who, instead of being supportive, takes every chance to one-up your story by saying something more dramatic or more interesting.

While I was driving to the clinic, she asked where I was going. I told her my whiplash-in-my-sleep story, which I thought was kind of unique. I wasn't trying to elicit sympathy, just answering her question. Without acknowledging my injury or even skipping a beat she replied, "Did I tell you I broke my ribs before?"

Even being aware enough to recognize Top-It as a communication condition, I still felt like saying, "Yep, 50 times; now back to me." I didn't.

To understand the game of Top-It, imagine a friend, who says, "I'm having a bad day." Person B responds, "Really? I'm having a horrible day. What happened to you?" Person A replies, "I missed a deadline for a project and my boss was upset." Then B goes on, "That's nothing. I got stuck in traffic, forgot my laptop at home, blew the sales presentation, spilt coffee all over my shirt and the boss embarrassed me in front of everyone." The implication is that B's problems are more important than A's. In fact, they both had a bummer of a day.

Top-It players may not mean to do what they're doing. Topping your story may begin as an attempt to show empathy, but like in the example above, it backfires. It made Person A feel insignificant and minimized her problems as if they are less valid. Person B risks coming across as insecure, because he hangs his identity on always having the better tale to tell.

Another friend is also a master at Top-It. Barely a conversation ends without at least one anecdote of how he has done the same thing better, bigger or more times than someone else. It's very frustrating for anyone who is trying to make conversation with him. I bet people would respond to him much better if he would just stop trying to have the best story in the room.

Trying to outdo each other's bad experiences by playing Top-It is not helpful. I notice this a lot when I speak with other pain patients. It's one of the reasons I just couldn't keep going to pain support groups at the hospital. Ten of us would sit around a big table and a third of them would be trying to prove their traumas were worse than yours—as if having the worst pain deserved a trophy. The irony is that if your pain really is the worst, you lose.

Everyone has pain, be it physical, emotional, mental or spiritual. It's easy to judge from afar and say, "*Oh, that wasn't so bad. Anyone could deal with that. If Allison only knew what I am going through. My life is so much worse.*"

I get it.

I resisted writing this book because I feared readers might think my adversities are lightweight in comparison to theirs. Then I realized that's not the point.

Playing Top-It in your mind while reading my story or while listening to anyone else's is a sure-fire way to put up defenses and block valuable insights and understanding that could help move you forward. Playing Top-It can reduce your resiliency and harm your quality of life.

In no way is this book a "poor me" story. I don't want sympathy. I don't want to wallow in or rehash all the bad things that happened. If I could share my lessons without diving into my actual story, I would feel less exposed. Plus, I'm sure my mom would be much happier.

My goal for telling my narrative is not to negate yours. In fact, by being open and honest about my journey through the ups and downs of life and business, I hope to validate your situation and inspire you to thrive despite your struggles. I know you have a story – an important one.

Pain is subjective. Your injuries, regrets and grief can only be interpreted by you. Just because someone had a seemingly worse or better experience doesn't make your experience suck any less.

I'm also aware of and thankful for the many blessings that counterbalance the traumas in my life. I was born into a small-town middle-class family, with two loving parents and a brother who I count as one of my best friends. I have treasured friends I met as a child and I have some innate talents that allowed me to create a rewarding career even though I was limited to working part time during my decade of hell.

Some could suggest that having all of those blessings makes it much easier for me to become a Resiliency Ninja. Not so.

The principles it takes to be a Resiliency Ninja are basically the same, applied at varying intensity, no matter the type or extent of your problems. There will always be circumstances that have the potential to stall your life; comparing them to other people's stories doesn't change that. Regardless of your various challenges, you need to get up in the morning and perform at work the best you can. We're all tested in different ways.

It can try your resolve to keep it together in a sales meeting after earlier that morning your child screamed, "You're the meanest mom/dad ever. I hate you." Just as it will take inner strength to shine in a sales meeting after a cancer diagnosis, with a sick parent in the hospital or anything in between.

While my blessings may be obvious, you have them too, even if you can't immediately see them or feel like you've been shortchanged. There are always blessings to empower you.

Playing Top-It adds an unnecessary layer of annoyance to any dilemma. Avoid the temptation and bring your best self to focus on your friends' situations and provide the empathy they need.

Then there is the opposite of Top-It: Diminish-It.

A friend confided in me that she thinks her life has been too mundane because she hasn't been tested by big adversities. She thinks she can never really excel as a public speaker because she doesn't have a story of tragedy to share.

My first thought was how fortunate for her that she's been spared the deep lows.

My second thought was that she absolutely has gone through challenging times; she's just diminished her woes.

This approach is called minimizing. Sometimes it's a result of blocking negative experiences or numbing out the pain. When you need to power through and be ON for work or for your family, playing Diminish-It can be a useful technique. I'll teach you how to do that a little later. The problem is that diminishing your problems doesn't work for the long haul. Eventually you'll need to recognize and accept your struggles for exactly what they are, not more or less.

You may notice that I'm really good at minimizing. In fact, after reading an early draft of this book, my friend told me that it seemed like I was totally okay with the heavy times I've been through. She felt I was just skating through all the ups and downs. I wish. I was a mess during the hardest times. I often collapsed behind the scenes. It's easy to forget the devastation you've been through after you've done the work to come to grips with tragedy and dissolved all the negative associations. Apparently, I got so good at smiling while I was in misery that I ignored the fact I was playing tennis with boulders of hurt flying at me. I became a Diminish-It pro.

Diminish-It can sometimes come across as martyrdom, which is very frustrating and annoying. Declaring, *"Oh I'm fine,"* when you clearly have every right to be absolutely devastated will not serve your healing. Instead, acknowledge that right now your heart is ripping out and you need some time to deal with the current circumstances. There is no judgment in that. If there is, you'll need to find more empathetic friends.

I think early in life we are taught to dry the tears and ignore the pain as if distracting from the hurt makes it disappear. I believe this is the root cause of Diminish-It and the inability of most people to effectively communicate and deal with their negative emotions. It starts with someone, a parent, teacher, babysitter or anyone of influence, telling a kid to, "Suck-it-up and stop crying." Kids are taught to deflect pain from a skinned knee or a stolen toy. Over time they use the diminishing technique to pretend to ignore bigger issues like being bullied. Next thing you know, they're deflecting the pain from a sexual assault or a death in the family.

Diminishing pain doesn't mean the devastation goes away; it just teaches people to bury negative emotions quickly before they've had a chance to properly process them. People learn to deflect the parts of reality they don't want and create a habit of skating over the horrible, gut-wrenching emotions that are valid parts of living. If we honor these experiences fully, the toughest stuff will pass more quickly rather than lingering inside us, ignored and festering under the surface.

The common advice to stop crying and forget the pain is often given, I believe, because people don't want to see their loved ones suffer. When others suffer, they feel it too and that hurts. If those who are suffering stop crying or expressing their agony, it's easier for others to avoid embracing it or empathizing. It's the old "out of sight, out of mind" mentality, causing one to move prematurely to a place of pretend acceptance. Short-term comforts win over long-term healing.

The cure for Top-It and Diminish-It is to acknowledge circumstances as they are and to listen to yourself or others intently without judgment and comparison. Instead of falling into the suck-it-up-buttercup trap, allow time to process those undesirable feelings, which are perfectly valid.

Once you recognize how these games are played, you may, as I did, start to notice your own unhealthy patterns of playing Top-It and Diminish-It. Be aware of these even when you're just trying to help others.

My work as a business growth consultant has honed my ability to see problems and make recommendations quickly. That talent doesn't translate well to personal relationships when friends are suffering. While clients pay for and expect my guidance, friends may not be interested in solutions quite yet, or ever. Ultimately, I found that my friends feel more supported when I simply acknowledge their adversity rather than offer advice before they're ready to hear and accept it.

Realizing a friend is just venting rather than seeking advice allows for healthy empathy and support. It takes a lot of self-awareness and self-restraint to hold back fix-it ideas until friends in need request solutions.

At some point, a friend will be ready to go into solution-finding mode. At that time, go for it, start brainstorming, offer suggestions. Some people get there faster than others. Stereotypically men tend to look for solutions sooner than women, but I don't buy into gender assumptions. I know plenty of men who love to vent and lots of women who like to focus on fixing things right away. It's determined by the individual and by the circumstances.

Awareness of the human instinct to solve problems can help you when you're communicating to others. If they start to go into advice-giving mode before you're ready, consider starting your conversation by telling them you just want to vent. This will set the stage for a more supportive interaction.

Being a pro at playing Top-It can tempt you to magnify your circumstances and lead you to exaggerate your stories. On the other hand, playing Diminish It can tempt you to ignore your issues. Both habits pour more fuel on your problems. Adversity is strong enough. You can own your power by seeing your adversities exactly as they are, not worse or better than they are, and not in comparison to anyone else's problems.

Resiliency Ninja Formula

Self-Awareness +

Strength (♡ Heart + Mental + Physical) +

Resourcefulness = Resiliency Ninja

 Is it your instinct to compare your circumstances to someone else's and if so, do you tend to play Top-It or Diminish-It?

 How do you react when someone shares a problem? Do you listen and empathize, or do you go directly into solution-finding mode?

 Were you taught to stop crying before you had processed a hurt? If so, you may tend to play Diminish-It and skim over valid hurts.

 Your hurts are your hurts and comparing them to others will not serve your healing. Your hurts are valid.

 When friends share their problems just listen. Resist the urge to offer solutions before they are requested.

 Explain you just want to vent if you are not ready to hear advice from a friend.

 Brainstorm and make a list of all the blessings you have in your life. Include your supporters, your capabilities and your successes. Recall this list of gifts when you are feeling low or starting to teeter between being positive and negative.

4

Cascading Dominoes of Adversity

FOR A GAL WHO DOESN'T like to wallow in her troubles, I'm about to lay out a problem-laden path that is going to sound ridiculous. Seriously, I'm already rolling my eyes. If I hadn't lived it, I wouldn't believe it. Each hardship is bad enough on its own, but when they come in bunches the compounding effect makes such challenges harder to overcome.

To give you a high-level sense of what forced me to become a master at eliminating excuses and powering through, here is the abbreviated version of my decade of hell. While these next two chapters are more focused on my saga than I would normally be comfortable with, I realize that you need to know what happened to me so you can appreciate how I came to develop the ideas I'm sharing in this book.

The goal is to give you some context as to my life before, during and after the fan powered on high and why I was forced to become a Resiliency Ninja. I hope you will see parallel elements in your own challenges. Perhaps you too have been in a place where it feels like the gut-wrenching blows won't stop.

So here goes…

To pinpoint the beginning of my quest for resiliency isn't easy. Things started to turn sour when my father died on January 12, 2005, but I think my string of adversity-overwhelm really started on March 5, 2007. That's the day that physically the universe told me to stop. That day I had a botched surgery that damaged my two main pelvic nerves, causing relentless neuropathic pain. I went in for a simple cyst removal and ended up with a life of pain and additional surgeries to try to fix the consequences of the first.

Neuropathic pain is unlike bone or soft tissue pain. It's in a category all its own. Even so, it doesn't need to be a life sentence.

My main post-surgical pain can best be described this way. Be forewarned, it sucks. Imagine taking the tip of a serrated knife and making an incision into your pubic bone. Wait 24 hours for the wound to start to heal and scab. Just as your brain begins to adjust to the pain and you relax, stick that same serrated knife back into the open wound. This time go deeper and start twisting repeatedly and aggressively.

Never stop twisting.

That's my one neuropathic pain. There are three additional pain sensations that range from numbness, to electric shock to a general sense of overwhelming brokenness that happen in unison around the surgical site. Those pains continue just as the nerve pain does.

That event changed my lifestyle significantly. I went from working power-packed, 16-hour days between business, volunteering, politics, networking and fun, to being confined to horizontal for often 20 or more hours a day.

It was a devastating blow. I felt trapped at home, wishing to be out in the community and wondering what I was missing. At that point my career was humming. In addition to being involved politically and raising money for charities, I had finished a contract as the founding executive director of an eating disorder support organization and wrote a popular column called the *People You Know* for the London Free Press. It was my job to create commentary around the who's who and the goings-on about the city four times a week.

I was just getting my footing after Dad's death and had already conquered a lack of self-confidence, my own eating disorder and some dreadful experiences with men. Finally, I felt like I had successfully overcome so much and started to see the world as my oyster. I was playing big in a small pond and I loved it. I was just on the brink of expanding my sights beyond the city where I lived.

I launched my company, Elevate Biz, just four months before the surgery that caused the damage. The plan was to leverage my newly acquired networking talents to teach others how to connect with decision-makers. I'd come a long way from my days as a receptionist and bartender and I'd worked relentlessly to get there. Thanks to my extensive network, my business was off to a strong start. Training and coaching clients were flying in the door. "Wow," I said to myself. "This consulting thing is easier than I thought."

Not so fast.

My momentum came to a screeching halt after the surgery. Physically

I was in uncharted territory and I didn't have my Resiliency Ninja skills developed at that point. The best I could do was function on adrenaline when I was expected to be "on", and then collapse behind closed doors. "Resume the position" (on the couch) was the joke among my closest friends.

The best way to illustrate my shift in lifestyle is to consider my tolerance for crime shows on TV. Pre-surgery, if I watched a police drama I was so scared, I would have had all the lights on and kept checking outside, even though the curtains were closed to be sure the boogey-man wasn't lurking in the shadows. My fingers were hovered over the fast forward and mute buttons just in case.

Post-surgery, confined to the couch for more hours than I want to admit, I became numb to even the scariest shows. When you see hundreds of episodes, you tune out to the gruesomeness. I'm not sure that's a particularly positive result from all that down time, but it goes to illustrate how much time I spent numbing out from the world. If I didn't have to be on, I was completely switched off.

A week after my operation, a good friend came over with some nachos for a visit. Sweet, but even my favorite comfort food couldn't relieve my extreme pain. The pain killers were barely scratching the surface.

I told him the harrowing tale of my extended surgery. I also told him about the nurse who wheeled me into the driver's seat of my car to drive myself home from the hospital just 20 minutes after another nurse had given me an intravenous bag of narcotics and drowse-inducing Dramamine. How bad must the healthcare system be for a patient to be forced to drive an hour home post-surgery, post-meds, because "they needed the hospital bed?" This had me pretty pissed off. I wanted to do something about it.

My friend jumped up and down and started saying I needed to run for political office. It wasn't the first time someone had suggested that. Being a young professional with the ability to communicate and a passion for politics, it was a natural fit. Until that night I always had a reason to say no. As I tried to fall asleep, I couldn't think of one.

The next day I went to a meeting to help organize a political fundraiser. Many of my mentors were in the room. Sitting wasn't possible yet, so I stood for the whole meeting, leaning on the back of a huge black chair in the law firm's boardroom. After the meeting, I broached the subject of running for the nomination as a local candidate in the upcoming election. It was a very preliminary conversation, or so I thought.

When I left for home, the breaking news on the car radio was surprising,

"This just in, Allison Graham is seeking the nomination to run for political office." Baptism by fire: this was real, I was all in. Scared to death, I had no time to think of the physical realities of my situation. I spent the next two months going back and forth between lying on my couch and making calls asking for political support and votes in the nomination race.

At that time, I knew only the severity of the pain; I had no idea of its permanency. I naïvely assumed the debilitating sensations would be gone in a few weeks. At least, that's what the doctor told me when he dismissed my early complaints and prescribed me more pain pills.

Five days before the nomination vote, I went in for a second surgery to try to fix the mess from the first. Looking back, I have no idea why I trusted the same Surgeon Scissorhands again, but I did. That decision alone reminds me how I didn't advocate for myself back then in a way that served my needs.

Thankfully, I had Mom as my driver for surgery number two. No big deal, I thought, it can't be worse than the last time. I'll be back on the campaign trail in 24 hours and ready for Tuesday night's speech.

Again, not so fast.

The surgery itself seemed to have gone as planned, but in recovery we realized something wasn't right. Despite several requests from the nurse, the doctor refused to come back to the recovery room to check my incisions. She was concerned with the worsening bleeding, but ultimately shrugged her shoulders and discharged me to go home.

By the time we got home the bleeding seemed extreme. Blood was gushing out of me, soaking through eight paper towels in minutes. There are not enough crime shows in the world to prepare you for watching that much blood pouring out of your own body. Since the doctor had said the bleeding was normal before we left the hospital, Mom and I kept justifying it. As I lay in bed, Mom insisted I call the provincial Telehealth help line to make sure this was normal. Thank God, I did. The nurse who answered my call told me to go to the emergency department immediately. It turned out the doctor had nicked an artery and I was at risk of bleeding out.

In the middle of the night I woke up in a different hospital feeling like my body weighed a thousand pounds. I'd lost a lot of blood, but as a healthy, young adult, the doctor figured I would rebound quickly.

Meanwhile, my political team was stuffing envelopes and getting the final communication materials ready before Tuesday night's vote. Late nights are typical in campaigns and I was up against a longstanding formidable opponent. Just because I was in the hospital and down some blood didn't mean the campaign could stop. While I wasn't allowed to leave the hospital, I did insist I take a call at the nurses' station to talk with the team. What choice did I have?

Five days later I nailed my speech and won the nomination, which was cause for a huge celebration. It was not an easy race to win especially since I had just gotten out of the hospital.

Pushing my body and staying physically tough was a necessity. It was only possible because I was emotionally committed to the cause and mentally prepared to do whatever it took to get the job done. Heart strength and mental strength can overpower physical weakness.

Then the public political campaign began.

A lot of emotional pain comes from being a political candidate. Continuous, insensitive personal and political attacks mean you need to have thick skin to run for office.

In 2007 social media was just catching on in the mainstream, but even then, the lynch mob could find you. I think sometimes people forget that candidates are human beings, with feelings and families.

There were friends who refused to talk to me because of my political stripes. One said, "Talk to the hand, I have no use for your existence anymore." Just imagine that two weeks earlier he and I had enjoyed lunch together.

I kept a poker face and tried to look unscathed by such comments at the time, but I quickly realized how thin my skin really was.

Politics by itself is exhausting. Running for office while you're in pain is excruciating. Being a political candidate, being in pain and still running a start-up business? Well, you be the judge. How do you think that played out for me? I'll admit there were some tough days. Even so, on the outside I kept up appearances with a smile on my face.

Adding to the personal challenges of needing to quickly develop a thicker skin was the unanticipated financial strain of running for political office and pushing snooze on my business momentum. The campaign marked the beginning of my financial troubles.

Political candidates don't get paid for the months of campaigning leading up to the election. You only get paid if you win a seat in the legislature, but both my party and I lost the general election. Plus, I had new expenses that stretched the budget. By the end of it, my income had stopped climbing, my savings were gone and I'd started to accumulate debt. I'd resigned from writing my newspaper column after winning the nomination to avoid perceived conflicts of interest and since my pain was so bad I put the brakes on my new company for the duration of the campaign. My entire focus was playing the happy political candidate. Between my regular bills, my additional expenses, my shopping habit which I used to fill the voids in my heart and my limited physical capacity, a financial crisis was inevitable.

Money frustrations added a whole new set of pressures. Every day there was this dark cloud following me. It made me feel like an imposter. Here I was hanging out with the "movers and shakers" of my city, and yet, I had this mound of debt that felt insurmountable. It took a long time to work my way out of it, but I'm extremely thankful it's gone now. Even though carrying debt is common in North American culture, I had a deep sense of shame and embarrassment around my numbers. Compared to the average income, I was making a healthy amount of money. Even so, because of the lifestyle I chose to lead, some business deals that went sideways, and my lack of discipline around spending, my debts didn't go down for a long time. In hindsight, I could have spent less on stuff. The thing is, at the time, I was so longing in my emotional state that the tangible purchases filled a void that I couldn't even articulate let alone conquer. Only when I dealt with my heart and mental blocks did getting out of debt become easier.

After the general election, I crashed. The adrenaline wore off and I started to realize that my post-surgical repercussions were more serious than I thought. For several years, I managed small spurts of productivity each day with adrenaline peaks when I really needed to deliver a command performance. My new motto became: *"I can do anything for an hour, with a smile on my face, no matter how bad I feel."* I knew that if I just powered through, I would be rewarded with two or more days on the couch to recover.

For the first six years, medication did very little to offer relief. Many pills made me loopy from their side effects (I once fell asleep while talking to a prospect), so I couldn't stick with one medication for long. Some patients love the sensations of being 'stoned.' I don't. When you can't find a way to relieve the pain through traditional methods, the skills of a Resiliency Ninja become even more critical. Following the formula allowed me to excel in business and maintain appearances even though the pain was excruciating every day.

Eventually I found pain meds that gave me back a more standard working day with minimal side effects. I spent five years with a daily pain score of seven or eight out of 10, with severe peaks to 10. Eventually I stabilized around the five level which allowed me to resume a more normal social life. Accomplishing this was still very difficult. Today, after nearly a decade in nerve-pain hell I have improved to an average two or three out of 10 with random spikes to the top of the scale once or twice a day. This is still painful, but because I can dissipate the pain faster, it's much more manageable. This improvement may give pain patients hope that one day your pain, too, may subside. I lost that hope for many years as I bought into the theory that the intensity would stay forever.

Two years after the original surgery and more than a year after my political run, my doctors recommended I adjust my lifestyle and go on disability. I was stunned. Here I was, this enthusiastic up-and-comer, and their answer to my situation was to give up on my dreams and wave a white flag of defeat?

Screw defeat.

My quest became to solve the mystery: How could I excel despite the current reality of my physical pain, financial restraints and emotional hurts?

If anyone has ever told you to give up and cave on your vision for your life, I hope you offered them some strong words to get out of your way.

Have you adopted limiting beliefs because of other people's perception of your circumstances? For example, how I believed for a long time that the intensity of my pain would never subside.

Heart strength and mental strength can overpower physical weakness.

You do not need to accept others' recommendations that you give up, take the easier path and embrace defeat. Screw defeat.

5

And the Dominoes Continue to Cascade

THE PHYSICAL DEVASTATION ALONE MADE it tough to run a business and maintain a professional and social network. Working full time was not an option. When you add in my emotional bruises, it's a wonder I was even standing upright.

But all this was just the beginning.

Weeks after my last fix-it surgery was performed, the mentor who changed my life by introducing me to the power of networking passed away. His name was Angus and he was notorious for bringing young professionals into the community. He always said, "I'll bring you to the table, but it's up to you what you're going to do with it." He was in his 80s. They say mourning is easier when the deceased is older, and in many ways, that's true, but Angus' passing was still a huge loss. It marked the end of his friendly hellos and notorious hugs at almost every event I attended. I felt guilty because I never truly told him in depth how much I appreciated his support early in my career; now I would never get the chance.

As I walked into his funeral reception, I got a call from one of my best friends, saying that her brother had died suddenly due to an aneurism. He and I had two dates planned earlier that week and I thought he had stood me up for both. It was tragic. I was crushed. I mourned the relationship we never had the time to explore. Even more, I was devastated for my friend and her family, who had lost this amazing young man. He was so full of *joie de vivre.*

A week later my former boss, the one who gave me my first professional job as a fundraiser for The Salvation Army's Red Shield Appeal, passed away suddenly. He had been one of my biggest cheerleaders both when I worked for him and when I announced my political run.

The next week my Grandma, my mom's mom, died due to complications after heart surgery. Once again, I felt the deep dismay and sorrow death brings to a close family. Soon after, the younger sister of one of my best friends died suddenly. I had watched her grow from toddler to mother. Her death broke my heart. The 2009 death streak culminated with a devastating blow when my cousin, a 40-year-old father of two lost his battle with cancer after fighting a brain tumor for more than a decade. For all those years, he had been a source of inspiration. Even with the cloud hanging over him and his immediate family, he lived a full life.

As you may imagine, this parade of death left me numb. I had become a zombie, and not the cool kind you'd watch in movies.

When I started to rebuild my social life after so many setbacks, I was met with yet another wave of bruises from the fickle fates thanks to several fluke injuries.

Have you ever screamed into the ether: "*Really? You want me to handle even more?*"

At a young professionals' curling night, someone behind me threw a rock that struck me without warning, knocking me off my feet. I dropped to the ice, landing on both wrists. For the next several weeks I wore a cast on each arm, making even the basic elements of life such as eating, typing and getting dressed an annoying struggle.

Then there was my collision with a railing at a Pearl Jam concert. Rushing to the bathroom during the encore, I couldn't see the railing in the middle of the aisle because it was covered by a black curtain. My pubic bone and the corner of the railing collided at full speed giving me my next glimpse of the agonies of hell.

The swelling and bruising took six weeks to subside. Thankfully, the venue reworked the railings and curtains to avoid further injuries.

The mishaps continued. One day, after a few laps in the pool, I was texting and walking in wet flip flops when I tripped and flew big-toe first, into a set of cement steps. The hint of a hairline fracture meant a walking cast for weeks. I hope you never find out how much a big toe can hurt.

Then there was a skiing accident that left me with a partially torn knee ligament and a broken wrist after a skier ran into me and forced me into the trees. I didn't think anything could hurt more than my nerve pain, but a partial tear in the knee ligaments offered an intense jolt I hadn't felt until that injury. They say a full tear is less painful and easier to treat. The physiotherapy added another roster of medical appointments to my already crowded schedule.

Then I broke my nose in a freak accident while I was changing a tire on a NASCAR racing car. It was part of an amazing pit-crew exercise for the leadership team for my professional speakers' association, which I'll share more about later. Thousands of professionals have successfully participated in this experiential-learning exercise created by one of my colleagues. Leave it to me to be one of only two people to ever get hurt doing it. It was my job to change two of the tires. I chose that role because I loved the idea of using that high-speed drill to loosen the bolts. It just sounded cool. The problem was I didn't have the upper body strength to lift the tire onto the bolts from a kneeling position. Just as I finally maneuvered the tire onto the bolts, a friend, not realizing it was already on, tried to help by nudging the tire with his foot. He meant well, but in doing so he kicked the tire off the bolts—and it landed on my nose. Two surgeries later, my nose is still not back to normal.

Those are some of the obvious challenges people could see me coping with; it's hard to miss the casts, splints and wobbles. What wasn't as obvious was the impact that so many physical assaults had on my emotional well-being. Call it depression or a mild-form of post-traumatic stress disorder, but the cumulative impact of all these hurts and slow recoveries meant that staying positive and motivating myself to work required me to hone my skills as a Resiliency Ninja.

Over the years there were also hurts from lost friendships and family dynamics. Some of those stories will be revealed in the pages that follow. As will some of the stories about the men who came into my life and taught me some cruel lessons. It took a lot of healing efforts to trust men again and now that I do, I don't want to shine a light on the jerks who forced me onto the healing path. Those experiences generally preceded my decade of hell, so it's no wonder that, when I fell into my most vulnerable state, I was in no position to add an intimate relationship to the mix. I should mention there were also some thoughtful, incredible men along the way; we just weren't made for a long-term relationship together.

The point is, many heart-wrenching things happened to me in a very short period of time, and yet, I kept moving forward. My business survived and by many definitions, it thrived.

Whether you're an employee, a leader, a small-business owner with your own team or a solopreneur like I am, you too are likely to face fierce headwinds at any time. Being a Resiliency Ninja when the trouble is flying from all directions takes willpower and staying power.

The skills of resiliency are fully accessible to you. It doesn't matter what your story is, it's all about how you handle the problems you can't control.

Resiliency Ninja Formula

Self-Awareness +

Strength (Heart + Mental + Physical) +

Resourcefulness = Resiliency Ninja

How would you rate your staying power in tough times? Do you tend to power through or retreat?

Resiliency requires staying power.

The habit of resiliency is accessible to you. It's your choice how you react to circumstances out of your control.

6

Married My Mom

As you know by now, I did not literally marry my mom or even birth a dog. We all find comfort where we can.

A spouse is often referred to as your significant other. In my life, the most significant person has been, by far, my mother.

I believe that life always balances hardships with blessings. You must be willing to look for them or you won't notice the positive, equalizing forces around you.

During a shit-storm you have two options. The easy answer is to lie down and let things pound all over you. The second option, harder but better, is to keep running and find shelter. Mom and Winston were, in many ways, my shelter.

Considering the Resiliency Ninja formula (Self-Awareness + Strength (Heart + Mental + Physical) + Resourcefulness) calling my mother into town was me being resourceful. Calling on her also assisted with my heart strength, but that wasn't an expected outcome at the onset.

In 2009, in addition to grieving, I was desperately trying to find a way to make my nerve pain disappear. I had an incredible team of doctors, all of whom were empathetic, but their best efforts didn't mean there was a solution. In one particularly heated doctor's appointment, I was a blubbering mess. I bitched about all the personal and professional limitations that my pain was causing. It was decided I could no longer risk driving long distances on my own. That limited my service offerings since most of my clients were at least two hours away. Another suggestion was to cut my losses, stop fighting the fight and consider going on government disability until I was better able to cope. Who knew how long that would take?

That was a come-to-Jesus moment.

Even if the doctors hadn't brought up the suggestion that I go on disability leave, I knew something had to change. Adrenaline, sheer determination and a big smile were good short-term fixes, but they just weren't going to sustain me for the long haul.

I needed solutions ASAP. It was one of the many moments that inspired my path to becoming a Resiliency Ninja. I was ready to fight. The alternatives, to freeze or take flight were not desirable options for me. I was determined to find a way.

It's funny, but, as an adult, there is still an instinctive need, at least for me, to reach for a mother's comfort.

Being single, I had no one at home who could be that constant person for company or to pick up the slack when I wasn't feeling up to making dinner or couldn't even turn off the lights at night because I was too sore to reach the lamp. Mom became that person.

Mom, a retired school teacher, was living in the home I grew up in about an hour and a half from the city where I reside. Up until then we had a good relationship, but honestly, who wants to live with their mom when they're single and in their thirties? Plus, how many women want to go back to the full-time Mom role after being an empty nester for 14 years? Most people would probably say, "Love ya, but no thanks!"

Being one of the most generous souls I know, Mom dropped her life as she knew it and moved to London to help me. For the first few years she lived in her own apartment in the same building. We decided that between Winston and my travel schedule, it made more sense for us to live together in one house. Having someone else in my day-to-day life for the first time since I'd left home at 18 was an adjustment. Thankfully, it worked. Almost too well.

The "married my mom" joke started when I would listen to friends having conversations with their husbands. *What's for dinner? Can you stop at the store on your way home? How's your day going? What's the plan for the weekend? You won't believe what just happened.* All those day-to-day check-in conversations people have with their spouse were the same ones I was having with my mom. We debrief our days, share household tasks and plan meals and grocery shopping. She's my plus-one to family gatherings.

Eventually, I recognized Mom's role in my life was not just about caregiving, but also companionship. Trying to hide my constant pain from the people around me, while keeping up all appearances and running a business, was isolating. Mom was the only one who was privy to all the challenges I was facing. Her acceptance of my limitations was comforting. In front of Mom I didn't have to be strong and I didn't have to pretend everything was okay. I could hit my "off" button in the comfort of my own home and still know I wasn't alone. If she hadn't been here all those years, I can't imagine how I would have handled the sheer loneliness.

So, while I did not literally marry my mom, she became my rock, my companion and the company I needed to get through horrible days. When bad moments feel like they last forever, having a positive influence to support you can be the difference between staying afloat and sinking to the black depths of the ocean.

Unfortunately, it's often the people closest to us who get the brunt of our misfortunes and miseries. Many married friends admit that their spouses see them at their worst. Mom was no exception. I had to learn to not take my frustrations with life out on her. That restraint can be hard to achieve when the person who is waiting at home loves you unconditionally.

Now that I can turn off my own lights, drive myself to events out of town and have started dating again, Mom has had some health challenges, so we've reverted to more traditional roles. Even today, as I write this chapter, she is in the hospital with heart complications – yet she's editing chapters as I finish them.

Mom has edited every professionally published piece of mine, which equates to hundreds of thousands of written words, including multiple rewrites. That's a lot of editing. She was as excited and anxious as I was when my very first *People You Know* column ran on August 15, 2003. It was the morning after the Northeast Blackout, so I'll never forget that day. I was so nervous. I was relieved knowing people didn't have lights with which to read my first column.

You may be juggling full-time work while caring for aging parents. That's just one more layer of responsibility to add to your schedule. It's probably more relatable than having a parent come live with you to take care of you. I've lived with the stress of both roles – being forced back into "child" mode as an adult, and then thrust into the caregiver mode. Each has its own set of challenges and blessings.

I believe that it's as adults that we create the best, most fulfilling relationships with our parents, if we have the chance. I'm thankful I was given the opportunity to do that with my mom.

Resiliency Ninja Formula

Self-Awareness +

Strength (♡ Heart + Mental + Physical) +

Resourcefulness = Resiliency Ninja

 Do you take your frustrations out on the people closest to you?

 What steps, beyond recognizing your tendency, can you take to change this dynamic?

 Life balances hardships with a series of blessings, you just must be willing to see and appreciate them.

7

Birthed a Dog

NOW WHAT DO I MEAN by "birthed a dog"? If you're a pet lover, you may not need an explanation. If you don't love pets, you may not get it – but that's okay.

Before Winston, I used to laugh at people who treated their dogs like children. In fact, my brother and I spent a good deal of time teasing our cousin and her husband for dressing their dog and having a doggie car seat equipped with a water bowl and food dish. Ridiculous, I thought.

Be careful how you judge others for you may become the one who is judged. Well, laugh away, I love my little guy. Today I totally get the love one can have for a four-legged animal. They are fur babies.

For the record, I am not factually comparing nurturing a dog to raising a human. I know the difference. It's just a book title. One friend chastised me for comparing the two roles. She thinks I am being naive about what it takes to raise children. I think someone can't take a joke.

I admire those who have children and I recognize that balancing parenthood and work brings with it a whole set of challenges to which I can't yet relate. The guilt I feel going on business trips when Winston jumps into my suitcase and gives me those 'please-don't-go' puppy-dog eyes is enough to make my heart melt. Surely the tug only gets inconceivably stronger when it comes from a child who can talk.

I always hoped and expected I would be a mom. Growing up and through my twenties I wanted five kids! As the years passed, my desired number of children was forced to decline, but I still hope for at least two. That strong unrealized desire to be a mom added another layer of loss to the cascading dominos.

One day in 2009, after a doctor's appointment out of town, I called a friend to talk me through my pain while I was driving home. It had been a tough day.

My friend suggested I visit a nearby city called Stratford where there was a pet store with adorable puppies that were bound to cheer me up. At the same time as she made the suggestion, serendipitously, I saw the sign for the Stratford exit. I had no doubt that I needed to pull off the highway and go looking for some furry love.

As I walked into the store, it was obvious where the dogs were. There were large wooden bins painted white, each about four-feet wide by four-feet deep, aligned along the far-left wall. There were about five booths in that row, then several along the back wall and an equal number jutting out on the right to form a U-shaped area dedicated to finding your perfect pooch.

My first stop was at the first bin on the left where I picked up some of the Chihuahuas, then I went to the next bin and the next. Holding the dogs lifted my spirits a little, but there was no profound emotional impact. By about the fifth bin, I figured it was time to head home and planned to skip the remaining bins that were between me and the door.

As I started to leave, I noticed this little black bundle of fur curled up in the corner of the last white bin. The lone Shih-poo in the mix of other 8-week old black puppies, he was busy licking his paw, minding his own business and then, with a big lick, his head lifted. Our eyes met. In that instant, he started desperately scrambling his way towards me. He jumped over every other dog there, all of whom were oblivious to the fact that someone was coming their way. It's as if he gasped and tried to yell, "OH MY GOD, MY MOMMA! FINALLY! YOU'RE HERE!!"

By the time I reached the edge of the bin he had run up the little steps and was jumping my way. I caught him, literally midair, and there was no way I was putting him down.

An hour later we were on our way home. It was the best decision I've ever made.

Despite loving the freedom of running my own business, the trade-off was isolation. I spent a lot of time on my own creating material for my clients and focused on my healing. My peer group could not relate to the challenges of a one-woman show especially when the one woman was going through so many blows. My clients weren't privy to my ongoing struggles, which was the professional approach even if it made me feel inauthentic at times. Throw in injuries, pain, grief and depression, and that loneliness is magnified. Having this bundle of love and joy in my home, and a focus for my maternal instincts, made that time more enjoyable and purposeful.

It also alleviated some of the disappointment of not having children in my early thirties when many friends were starting families.

The "birthed a dog" joke started when I was on the phone with a friend. She was trying to rally her toddler to get out the door while I was rallying Winston to get going too. Our secondary conversations were eerily parallel. She was saying the same things to her little guy as I was saying to Winston. "Come on, please hurry up and go pee-pee." "Let's put on your coat, one paw, two paw." "Come on, stop dallying, we're going to be late." It was official. My dog was like my child.

It was more than just those types of daily activities that inspired the phrase. It was this feeling that I was his everything. No matter what happens in my life, I have a responsibility to care for him. His unconditional love makes me pause and be grateful. I'm in awe of his personality and his little quirks that make him who he is. Even watching him do the most mundane things like eat or stretch out on his back for a nap, put a smile on my face. And so, I recognized that the expectations I'd had for my life had flown the coop and this, yes this – that I'd married my mom and birthed a dog – was my new reality. It was humbling, disappointing, terrifying and comforting all at the same time.

So, there you go. *Married My Mom, Birthed A Dog: How to Be Resilient When Life Sucks.*

The book just had to be written.

Resiliency Ninja Formula

Self-Awareness +

Strength (♡ Heart + Mental + Physical) +

Resourcefulness = Resiliency Ninja

If you were to turn your life into a book, what would your book title be?

Be careful how you judge others for someday you may become the one who is judged for similar circumstances.

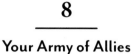

8

Your Army of Allies

THE PEOPLE WHO SURROUND YOU are your barrier to the outside world during the worst times. Going through adversity without the comfort of at least one person who has your back and knows the truth, would be extra difficult. Having the wrong people makes it even more so. Therefore, it's important to choose those allies wisely.

I imagine you sitting in the middle of a medieval castle. Your true friends are the guards who will shoot arrows from high atop the curtain wall to protect you when you come under attack. Some will stand watch all night at the mere mention that someone is about to storm your castle. There are others who will just ignore the attack and go about their own business, while some of the best allies will open a bottle of wine to help entertain you amidst pending doom. Then there are those who will abandon you by sneaking out before the drawbridge closes. Some may even join the intruding army's charge to attack, but most of those who flee will just disappear into the woods, never to be heard from again.

Unfortunately, you never really know who's who until you're staring into the blowing fan and dodging boulders flying at you.

In university, I read a book called *Choices with Clout* by Wilbur Cross. I still have my copy from 1995. While reading it, I realized I was making some bad decisions when it came to my social circle. This insight has stuck with me all these years. When I'm not showing up in my strongest, most authentic state I'll review with whom I've been spending the most time. My attitude and my business are both at their best when I connect with supportive friends who are accepting of me, forward thinkers who expand my vision and other entrepreneurs who challenge me. I'm most at peace when I spend time with low-drama friends who don't stimulate my flair for melodrama.

Have you noticed that different friends bring out different aspects of your personality?

You only need look to a motivational conference, where the music is pumping, the atmosphere is encouraging, and people are energized to reach their best self, to prove how the people around you influence your daily attitude. Making the decision to invest in attending a positive conference can fill you up like a helium balloon, but that's just the start. Be sure you plan ahead to combat the pending deflation which is bound to occur when you return home.

When I finished five days at a Tony Robbins' Business Mastery Seminar recently, I was spinning with enthusiasm. I was ready to serve the world. Then I came home and started talking with friends who hadn't been there. Some supported my enthusiasm while others resented it; they were just downers. Talk about stomping on my passions.

Thankfully, my working group from the seminar had committed to bi-weekly conference calls to hold each other accountable and ensure each of us maintains our momentum. It's because of these colleagues that I'm able to stay focused on my greater purpose, ignore the cynics and maintain a positive, joyful attitude.

People will either pull you up or tear you down. Relationships can't keep you static. That's why it's so important to surround yourself with people who inspire you, who won't accept lame excuses and who truly want to see you succeed. They are the ones who have your back and will stand beside you without judgment through tough times. Choosing to spend your time with people who lift you helps you stay strong.

Identify those who inspire you to stretch outside your comfort zone and become an even better version of your authentic self. Then spend more time with them.

Just as your family and friends can bring out the best in you, every person you're connected to has the potential to magnify your problems and make life harder. It's up to you to recognize the energy suckers, cruel schmucks and the passive-aggressive wolves in sheep's clothing and eliminate those people from your life – or at the very least minimize their impact.

How can you expect to flourish when the very people who are your family and friends are the ones throwing punches at you? They may not even know they're discouraging you, as they may feel they have your best interests at heart.

The friends you care immensely about may not be the same ones who bring out the best in you and vice versa. Friendships create patterns of communication, which means that sometimes it's not the people who are bad for each other, but rather, the rituals of engagement between two people that are unhealthy.

A conversation soundtrack is created every time people talk. It can be positive or negative. When you're caught in a glum cycle, being together is like holding hands and jumping into a black hole of pessimism. Nothing good can come from either of you tolerating that.

For example, if you and your friend are both single and continually reinforce each other's belief that there are no quality men who want strong successful women (or vice-versa) then shockingly, the two of you will likely stay single.

If your spouse thinks that success is reserved for the rich and that you're never going to make it and you buy into the philosophy, you will help each other self-sabotage every business you start to prove your beliefs right.

The brain delivers what you ask it to send.

The answer is not to delete all your uninspired family, friends and colleagues from your life. Nor is it to blame them for your woes. Just protect yourself as best you can by limiting your exposure to toxic influences. Shield yourself from negative messages that don't serve you well. To do this, instead of just taking people's opinions at face value, sort through their comments to decide if you agree or not. You are not required to believe other people's opinions.

I have friends whose parents were very unsupportive about their career choices. After years of nagging and discouragement, my friends stayed their course and eventually their families accepted their choices. My friends chose not to let the people who didn't "get them" influence their path, even though they loved them.

You can't cut out all your negative contacts. There is a person whom I care deeply for, but I know that every time I call I need to be ready for a depressing conversation filled with complaints and regrets. There seems to be no end to her past-focused, excuse-laden rehashing of how horrible life is. But not calling is not an option.

So, I attempt to emotionally protect myself and counteract the negative influence. If not, I am at risk of becoming grouchy during and after the conversation, until I reset my energy. For a long time, I accepted her point of view as to how the world works, justifying her beliefs because she had suffered a lot of hard knocks. Eventually, as I started to recognize my own self-sabotaging patterns and became more positive about life, the conversations would turn into a fight because I was growing. She was basking in her destructive place.

Despite my best intentions, I finally accepted that it's not my responsibility to motivate her. Like you, I can only be responsible for how I react to situations and how I show up in a relationship. Instead, I just appreciate her as she is and tune out to the pity-party on the other end of the phone. I still offer support, but I've stopped using my positive energy to try to change hers. That's a no-win challenge.

The good news is you can change relationship ruts by adjusting your reactions and communicating your expectations. Calmly explain your desire to change the soundtrack, your vision for a positive future and your commitment to staying focused on what you can control, not wallowing in the past or fretting over issues you can't fix. The best friends are those who choose to walk this more positive path together, encouraging each other to see problems from an optimistic perspective.

One way to do this is to create a list of topics that are off the table for discussion. For example, there are a few friends with whom I know I will never agree politically, so why even broach the subject? Another difficult topic may be the whole concept of self-improvement. Not everyone understands your desire to become more thoughtful and purposeful about creating happiness and joy. Change can make some people fearful that, if you grow too much and become too successful, they will lose you. If someone is not supportive of your journey to continually improve yourself and your attitude, then avoid discussing the specific areas of growth that you are focussing on at that moment.

Another simple tactic for evolving your conversations is to change where you meet your friends and the activities in which you engage. Infusing a new sense of adventure can flip the script and enhance your connections and relationships.

You can also add a buffer friend to join you. If I find I've created a negative conversation pattern with a friend, then I will change up that dynamic by introducing a third or fourth person to the mix. Ultimately, we'll talk about more inspired ideas compared to when it's just the two of us wallowing in our well-worn soundtrack. This way, you can maintain close friendships while giving your conversations more room to roam. Plus, you'll have a new, more positive benchmark for your conversations when it is just the two of you again.

Protecting yourself from unhealthy relationships is not just about keeping a positive attitude. It's also about being sure you stay the best, most authentic version of you. Allowing negativity to creep into your life without recognizing it starts to take you down a dark path. This is in large part due to a psychological phenomenon called "mirroring." Humans are basically hardwired to imitate the attitudes, gestures and speech patterns of the people with whom they spend the most time. Mirroring is a great way to build connection, but it also means you're likely reflecting the people closest to you. Is that good or bad? Would you want to approach life through the same lens as the people you let into your day-to-day?

The mirroring effect of human nature is fascinating to me. I see how over the years I've picked up mannerisms from living with Mom that I didn't catch growing up, and vice versa.

Mom is a sweetheart and loves to tell stories. She's also exceptionally detail-oriented and this comes out in her long-winded tales that come complete with every background detail you would ever need – and many more you don't.

After a while I noticed that my own story-telling had shifted to include more random details that I would normally have skipped or skimmed. Once I started noticing this behavior, I could consciously revert to my own no-frills approach that makes me a more effective communicator for my personality.

Other areas that mirroring can influence include finances, exercise, business momentum, promotion chances, entertainment preferences and daily habits.

Being aware of who you're mirroring and what habits you're accidentally picking up can help you stop and change ways if these new behaviors don't serve your desire to be authentic, present and consistent.

I am so grateful for my incredible family and friends in my army of allies. Many have thrown virtual "fire bombs" to support me in my greatest times of need (as I have for them). Of course, Mom and Winston are two of my greatest allies, but by no means are they the only ones. There is a collection of men and woman who encourage me, offer insights and inspire laughter. The people who have helped me along my journey – in small or large ways – know who they are and that I appreciate them immensely.

One person who has been instrumental in helping me build my resiliency muscle is a psychologist who specializes in serving patients with severe chronic pain. Let's call him Dr. T. It took me a few years after the surgery to find him and when I did I was a long way from accepting my situation and was underliving my potential.

After years of appointments with Dr. T, I have learned to break destructive patterns and accept myself—pains, faults and all. His wisdom and patience have been invaluable resources. I learn something new from each visit. A lot of the coping mechanisms I share in this book have been influenced by my sessions with Dr. T.

In order to know who you can count on as you become a Resiliency Ninja, take note of your army of allies. Who is on the list? Have you told them how much you appreciate having them in your life? Sometimes it's the people closest to us who get forgotten. They are also routinely the people who see our worst sides. How many times have the people at home taken the brunt of your bad day at work?

Avoid sharing your troubles with dramatizers, 'catastrophizers', minimizers, criticizers, gossipers and basically anyone who makes you feel like you can't be your best self. It's not helpful when you go searching for advice and support then feel worse after you've confided in someone.

Choose your confidants wisely.

Self-Awareness +

Strength (♡ Heart + Mental + Physical) +

Resourcefulness = Resiliency Ninja

 Whose behaviors are you mirroring?

 Do you have a strong army of allies around you or do you need to complement your current circle with new, more positive friends?

 What are the positive and negative communication soundtracks that have been created with your friends?

 It is not your responsibility to motivate others; trying to help others who don't want your help will drain your emotions.

Tell your army of allies how much you appreciate and love them.

Sometimes it's not that the people are incompatible with you rather, it's the rituals of engagement between you that are unhealthy.

Change the patterns of interaction with friends by introducing new activities, locations for meeting and additional people.

Make a list of off-limit conversations with certain friends to break the patterns of destructive communication.

Find a therapist, mentor or coach who will guide you, without judgment and preconceived notions.

9

The Breaking Point in Friendships

SOME SAY A TRUE FRIENDSHIP can endure anything and will never go away. In my experience that's not the case. There is a potential breaking point in every relationship, and if you don't find it and fix it before it snaps, those ties will eventually be severed.

My friend and I were talking about this the other night over a glass (okay maybe a few glasses) of wine. We decided that friendships are akin to glassware. Every friendship has a certain capacity. Shot glasses have a smaller threshold than a champagne glass, which is smaller than a rocks glass, which is smaller still than the volume of a pint glass for beer. There are even a rare few with the capacity of a pitcher.

Friends are the same way. Unfortunately, you may not recognize a friend's capacity in your life until adversity strikes, their glass overflows, and they disappear.

People enter your life for a reason, a season or a lifetime. There are only a handful of individuals in each person's life who will truly have your back through thick and thin, without question, no matter what happens and forever. It's a treasured few who can withstand adversities without overflowing beyond their brims.

Longevity is not always the best indication of the depth of a friendship. I am proud to have cherished friends from kindergarten and grade school who still stay connected in a meaningful way.

There are many friends I met as an adult who I appreciate just as much. Of course, there were many who were once close, but for whatever reason, are no longer part of my day-to-day life. That doesn't mean we don't still care about each other.

It's natural for people to come in and out of our lives as circumstances change. This process can be heartbreaking or a cause for celebration.

I used to resent friends who would call me when they were single and then ignore me as soon as they hooked up with a partner. Chronically single and always happy to lend an ear, I am often the first person these disappearing friends call when their relationships end. While I will never understand why many couples rarely include their single friends in group outings, I finally learned to let go of my resentment and feelings of abandonment. The blow is cushioned by the acceptance that human nature is constantly changing. I still consider most of my coupled-off friends among my best friends, even though we no longer interact routinely. Our lives have simply evolved in different directions. Instead, I treasure the time we had together and thank them for the season.

As we get older it can feel harder to make new friends, so it's important to do all we can to hold onto the ones we have. Being aware of how much you're pouring into your relationships is a good start. When it comes to discussing hardships with friends, the relationship soundtrack needs to ebb and flow. You both need to feel celebrated in times of triumph and feel supported when you talk about your problems. The back-and-forth is healthy and satisfying.

Relationships are put at risk when one person's problems are constantly consuming all the airtime. In very difficult times, such as the death of a loved one, losing your job or suffering a major injury, then of course conversation will lean to one side. For a friendship to remain healthy, it needs to spring back to equilibrium sooner rather than later.

Leaning on friends for help is one of the most important and endearing aspects of caring for each other. But there's also a risk involved when you don't have the tools or confidence to solve problems on your own and you're constantly relying on someone else for answers. If the person you rely on is ever ripped away from you, what will happen then? You're lost. Or you replace that person with another relationship too soon, just to fill the void.

If you don't have someone beyond your closest friends who can guide you through difficult times, I encourage you to find someone right now. As I mentioned before, the right doctor, mentor or coach will support you without judgment and offer sound advice without preconceived notions of the perfect direction for your life. Friends aren't therapists. If you have the means, it's exceptionally valuable to hire a professional to listen to you process your stories and help you find your way in the worst of times. Often the advice you need is already inside of you, you just need someone to help you find your internal wisdom. It doesn't have to be a paid therapist; maybe it's a wise friend with an outside perspective who wants you to succeed and is not invested in specific outcomes.

If you love to talk through your problems, but can't afford a therapist (or even if you can), record your thoughts privately in a journal. This allows you to process your feelings and start to look at your issues objectively before you approach your friends and mentors for their opinions. Being able to work through your preliminary thoughts and feelings on big issues can save hours of talking with friends and advisors. People appreciate it when you come for advice with your facts sorted, and when they see you've already been working on forming your own answers.

When attacked by a group of foes, a Resiliency Ninja wouldn't stop to talk through his options. Instinctively he'd evaluate the situation and use the appropriate tactic gained through extensive prior study and experience.

No one solution fits all. You may have multiple advisors, because each person has a different lens through which they see your adversities and encourage you to rise to the occasion.

If it's a work-related problem, seek counsel from a person with credibility in your industry, or someone who is more successful than you. You won't be well-served if you get business advice from someone who has never run a prosperous company, or advice on how to land your next promotion from a co-worker at the same level as you. You won't learn how to manage difficult people from a person who attracts the most drama in his or her life. Instead, poll an accomplished business person, your manager or a human-relations specialist – those are most likely the people you can trust to guide you positively in related matters.

With all the punches that kept coming at me, as you can imagine, it was a bit much for some of my closest friends. It's probably why I felt such comfort with Mom, who kind of had to put up with me unconditionally.

I learned about capacity in friendships the hard way.

During my most difficult times personally, I was attracting the most public prominence in my life. I was active in the media, was running the eating disorder center, had started my company, and ran for political office. But in the background, I was dealing with all the problems I've shared with you.

Even though I was running a successful business and keeping up appearances, when I was in private and had switched off my "on" personality, my closest friends got the brunt of all my troubles. Some friends stayed by my side. Others just naturally faded away, some chose to leave abruptly, and some I left.

One dear friend whom I thought would be in my life forever got angry with me one day. I've never heard from her again. In a second, she severed the ties of our friendship. It was devastating on top of everything else that was happening. It was three days after the second funeral I attended in 2009. It turns out she was just sick of hearing about all my hard knocks and had reached her limit of what she could take on my behalf.

She'd known me through five surgeries and some bad breakups, now she was witnessing my grieving—again. She just wasn't taking any more. Between the grouchiness caused from my excruciating physical pain and my emotional heartbreak, she was done. In hindsight, I recognize I was a burden and was counting on her friendship much more than I could reasonably expect to.

Although I wish that the relationship had gone differently, I respect that friendships are not the places to constantly unload problems. They're friends, not therapists. This is one of the experiences that shaped my opinion that, if possible, you should hire a professional to coach you. At the time, I didn't have a psychologist to guide me and I'm sure that from my friend's perspective, she was being treated as an emotional dumping ground. It's a friendship I immensely regret losing.

A lesson learned. And I'm still learning.

Another cherished friendship was tested when I allowed my frustrations to influence my attitude to a waitress who was providing poor customer service at the local movie theater. Being rude to people is a trait I've long considered a no-no when it comes to your reputation management. So, you can imagine that when I am off my game in public, there must be something terrible going on in the background.

Earlier that day I had been to a fertility clinic. I was trying to figure out if I could still have children and ascertain what the impact of my pain would be on carrying a baby. Although I was diagnosed as healthy, no one could tell me if the pain medications would affect a fetus. There was no research on the impact of the medication I was taking on children born into low-risk environments. The doctor's best guess was that my baby would be fine. He recommended that I should continue taking the pain meds. A mere guess wasn't a good enough answer for me, which is why I became focused on getting off medications and testing my ability to function without the assistance of chemicals. After all, raising kids isn't something you can do from the fetal position under the covers.

So, needless to say, I was feeling grumpy, frustrated and resentful. Those emotions boiled over in an interaction with a Cineplex server who told me small popcorn bags were no longer available for purchase in the VIP area. If I was on the other side of the theater, I could buy a small-sized popcorn. How ridiculous. My friend was embarrassed by my snarky reply "OK, then fill a medium bag halfway," followed by a rant about the situation. It sounds silly, but that was the breaking point: the end of an eight-year friendship.

It wasn't the popcorn. It was the accumulated strain on a close friend who had lived through all my sorrows with me, sat in emergency rooms with me too many times, and was privy to the ups and downs of my business. It's too much to ask of any one friend, even a BFF.

You may be asking the same question I've asked so many times: How can you win? It's a Catch-22. If you don't share your problems with your friends, aren't you hiding your authentic self, creating superficial relationships? But if you lean on friends for everything that happens, you may become a burden, especially if you're suddenly buying tissues by the case.

There is no easy solution. The best answer I can suggest is that in any relationship, each person should contribute equal amounts of effort and sharing. My policy now is to filter the tough stuff. I rarely let anyone know everything and I make a point to notice if negative communication patterns are taking hold in my relationships. By noticing these behaviors, I can catch the unhealthy play-by-play early to avoid overwhelming a friend or to prevent us from jumping into the black hole of pessimism.

I think every friendship goes through up and down stages. For me, however, the adversities didn't seem to stop. Coping with all my troubles was hell for me, let alone for any friends who were by my side during my misery.

In this book I'm sharing many stories they would have lived through. The difference is I've worked through the emotional turmoil that goes with all the situations, so I can now talk about them from a place of hope and confidence. I don't need the talk therapy any more.

In both cases mentioned above, my friends were very supportive until they just couldn't take it any longer. Our friendship pattern was that both of us talked too much about the disappointments in our lives. I was not the only one who faced challenges. But as much as we took comfort in unloading our frustrations on each other, neither of us used that shared experience to cheer up, get better and stop wallowing in the bad.

There have also been times when I decided that I had to let go of a friendship. Sometimes the patterns we created just weren't healthy. I ultimately decided I couldn't be someone else's punching bag. I used to find it hard to set, and stick to, boundaries for how I wish to be treated. Eventually I realized that if I didn't set the standard of respect, people would just make their own rules. There were times when that was OK, but other times when it was not.

Think of your own friendships. Are you placing too many emotional expectations on others? Are you continually revisiting the same tragedies and never moving forward? If so, consider resetting the communication patterns as soon as possible, so you don't lose people you care about as I did.

Resiliency Ninja Formula

Self-Awareness +

Strength (Heart + Mental + Physical) +

Resourcefulness = Resiliency Ninja

 Do your friendships have a balance of give and take or do you place too many burdens on other people?

 Longevity is not the best indication of the depth of friendship.

 Friends aren't meant to be therapists.

Friendships evolve and that's okay. Each person comes into our life for a reason, a season or a lifetime. Honor that.

Start processing your problems in a journal. Rereading what you've written gives you a new perspective on your thoughts and can help you find answers before reaching out to a friend.

10

Better Single than Unhappy

IF ONE MORE PERSON ASKS me why a beautiful, successful woman like me is still single, I'm going to scream. A full-on, horror flick, operatic-high-note-that-won't-stop kind of scream. Right on the spot, I'm just going to let it all out.

If they follow that question by asking, "Is it because you're intimidating to men?" I'll take another deep breath and keep screaming. I may start stomping my feet and flapping my arms in protest too.

These are the two worst questions to ask a person who is single. It's like asking a married couple why they haven't had babies yet – when you don't know whether they've had miscarriages, or are devastated they can't get pregnant, or just don't want kids.

These sorts of useless, passive-judgmental questions need to stop.

The question "Why are you single?" is so hurtful because it insinuates that somehow you are "less" because you haven't yet walked down the aisle. You're not "less" just because traditional society expects you to find a mate and the fact that you haven't done so requires an explanation.

I know a true life partner will go through everything with you, but I didn't want to get serious with a man and subject him to my many sorrows and afflictions. As I reflect, there's one answer to the "Why am I single?" question.

Still, how can we talk about bouncing forward from tough times without acknowledging the profound influence a significant other has on one's life? It doesn't take a relationship expert to see that choosing the wrong mate magnifies life's problems. Longing for your partner to offer you support that he or she isn't capable of giving is yet another boulder blowing through the fan blades of life.

Here's what I know for certain: I would prefer to be single and happy than miserable in a relationship with the wrong guy. Today's sky-high divorce rates lead me to believe that choosing the person with whom to build a life together is a decision not to be taken lightly. There are too many people who feel stuck in unhappy marriages.

Waiting till you find the right person may mean waiting longer, but I believe it is worth the wait. The person I am now is significantly different from the person I was at 30, and because of that I know I'd be a much better mate today for the right guy. Rushing into the wrong relationship back then, especially given the calibre of men I was attracting at the time, would not have been a healthy decision.

During my most difficult times, it was too much to even consider adding a new serious relationship to my bundle of burdens. My focus was survival. Physically it wasn't even an option. But now it's a different story, so I've turned my attention back to relationships and started dating again. I can see why I found it easier to be single rather than married all these years. Dating can be uncertain and adding a traditional significant other into your life adds a new variable that keeps you on your toes and can add to life's challenges and blessings.

Going through hard knocks tests a couple's faith and fortitude, and I wanted to be sure I could show up with confidence in a relationship, so I could do my part to get through the lows. Earlier in my story, I just didn't have the tools to do that.

It takes a lot to trust that another human being will love you even when you're not capable of being your best self. I've since realized that the truest bonds of love are forged in the most imperfect times, provided each person is willing to be vulnerable and committed to each other.

I've seen too many kind men and women falter in their relationships when their partner isn't at their best – whether due to job loss, grief, weight gain, depression or any other challenge. When couples make their "for richer and for poorer, in sickness and in health" commitment, I think many, not all, are prepared for the good parts, but assume the bad will be quick and painless. It rarely is. When the pressures get too much they stop communicating and that can be the beginning of the end. Marriage is hard enough, especially as couples grow in new and often separate directions.

A good friend of mine has been married for more than 30 years. She says the secret to her successful marriage is that each partner wakes up every morning and focuses on how they can make the other's life better. They are committed to serving each other's best interests. Early in their relationship, she decided to make sure that coming home from work would be the best part of her husband's day. No matter what problems she had to report, when he walked through the door he was greeted with a warm smile, a loving kiss and a friendly tone. It works for them and I think it's a good way to maintain a relationship.

Cohabitating with Mom as an adult taught me the comforts of coming home to someone who is caring, sympathetic and supportive no matter what. I wouldn't wish for anyone to walk into their home and feel unsafe or unsupported. So, if you're stuck in a toxic relationship I encourage you to get professional advice, to figure out how to change those circumstances, or how to trust yourself enough to be single. Being alone is not the worst thing that can happen to someone. Feeling lonely or scared when you're in an intimate relationship would be unbearable.

I watched a Tony Robbins video in which he talked about how he met his second wife Sage. He wrote six pages about what he was looking for in a mate, including what the relationship would feel like, what they would do together and what kinds of conversations they would have. Then he narrowed his list down to three pages. Next, he flipped the script and asked himself, "What kind of a man do I need to be to attract a woman of this calibre?" He focused his efforts on becoming that man. Soon after, he met Sage.

Tony's focus struck a chord with me, and I've been going through the same process since I watched the video. I'm having a blast becoming the person I believe will attract the right man. It's a much more joyful state than wondering if my guy is around every corner. If he doesn't appear, then at least I am having fun creating memories that I'll cherish. If he does, I'll be thankful I found such a fun path while I was waiting for him.

The same principle applies to anyone in a relationship. Finding and being the best version of you will encourage your mate to step up and reach his/her potential too. At least it stops the frustrations of trying to "fix" the other person – which if you've tried you know is an impossible task. We can only improve ourselves.

The types of people you attract into your life are influenced by what you believe you deserve. I have friends who continually choose partners who treat them poorly. When we dive into what's driving these choices, we find that at their core they don't *feel* lovable. Staying with someone who treats them just badly enough keeps them nicely anchored in their comfort zone. It's unsettling to have someone treat you exceptionally well if you don't think you're worthy of that level of kindness and love.

In talking with divorcees or bitter singles I get frustrated when they say things like, "The ones who are left are all assholes," or "All the good ones are taken." Painting all men (or women) with the same brush because you're not getting what you want, is like giving up apples forever just because you found one with a worm in it.

You'd miss a lot of great apples.

 Are you focused on trying to change your partner or find one, or on becoming the best version of you?

 How do you feel you deserve to be treated by a partner? Do you feel lovable?

 How can you serve your heart and love yourself in such a way that it inspires your significant other to love you the same, respectful way?

 Notice your patterns of thinking. Have you bought into negative stereotypes with regards to relationships or do you come from a hopeful place?

Does your home environment feel safe and supportive? How can you make it so?

Make an exhaustive list of everything you want from a relationship and focus your efforts on becoming the mirror image of that person you wish to attract.

11

Stuck in Quicksand

IMAGINE YOU'RE THE LEAD ACTOR in a cheesy movie from the 1960s, when it was popular to dramatize the unlikely risk of drowning in quicksand. You're running along the edge of a blue lagoon when you stop to take a sip from your water bottle. There you are, enjoying the view, when suddenly, you start to sink. You're in quicksand.

Thankfully the jogging group behind you catches up and sees what's wrong. They're quick to respond and throw you various life-saving tools they happen to have in their jogging packs, including a strong rope. They are ready and willing to pull you out of your troubles, but instead of wrapping the line around your waist, you just keep sinking. In fact, at one point you pull out a cigarette that you secretly hid in your fanny pack years ago – just in case. The cigarette is stale and it's not good for you, but you light it anyway. After all, you're drowning in quicksand.

Your rescuers are frantically calling from a safe distance, "Stop. Stop. There's a way out. Just grab the rope and you're free."

You hear them, you may even wave, but dammit, this dramatic tale of drowning is so fascinating you're staying put. The quicksand can't be that deep, you think. "I'll just wallow here for a bit, smoking my smoke and sinking slowly." You may even appease your onlookers by saying, "Yes, don't worry, I'll grab the rope soon." Secretly you're thinking, screw them, I won't give them the satisfaction of accepting their help.

So often we are thrown life-lines, yet we stay so focused on the quicksand below us that we can't see the bright future that will come from accepting help. To be resilient when life gets hard, you have to want to look up and see that the answers to your prayers are within arm's reach.

It's your responsibility to grab the rope.

Resiliency Ninjas first must be self-aware enough to notice the patterns and excuses that are keeping them stuck, and then find the strength and resources to pull themselves out of harm's way. How to get unstuck may not be immediately obvious (in later chapters you'll learn how), but if you don't choose to get out of the sinking sand, first, you're going to drown in a puddle of doom. This applies for any toxic situation in life, not just relationships.

It's often easier to spot repeating patterns in others. Have you ever called to a friend from the sidelines, desperately urging them to come to safety, and wishing they would stop stepping into toxic traps? Have you watched a friend repeating the same destructive behaviors at work, in relationships, or with their physical health? It's hard to listen to their excuses and justifications over and over as they spin their tales that one day the quicksand will magically change to solid ground. Have you watched a friend or co-worker stubbornly wallow in misery or grief, refusing to take the initiative to get better, while in the meantime, you're encouraging them to come out and play under blue skies?

Sometimes the person who is staying stuck is you.

One reason a person will stay stuck and drown is that she doesn't love herself enough to bother choosing a healthier path. She may say she doesn't want to hurt anymore, but she's quite comfortable polluting her lungs and going nowhere. Deep down, she probably believes she deserves to sink.

Another reason people might stay stuck is that they can't see their next steps clearly. In the absence of a clear direction, it's easier to freeze.

One puddle of quicksand where I found myself firmly stuck was with my business. The company I'd built served me well from a financial perspective, but lately, I hadn't been feeling fulfilled. I finally had the physical capability to ramp up my client work and yet I just wasn't inspired to do so. In fact, I was suddenly resenting it. At that point I'd earned a strong reputation as a "networking expert." After all, I had authored two best-selling books about networking which made me feel like I was tied to this topic. Clients and connections assigned me to the networking box when I ached to do more, and I hated it.

Sure, being able to successfully meet people and build your personal contact network is imperative in business and social life, and I was pleased to show people how to connect better, faster and more easily. But I was bored repeating the same content year after year. I needed to use more parts of my brain. I dreaded the idea of teaching people how to mingle, remember names and get more value from events for the rest of my professional life.

There were several things happening that contributed to keeping me stuck. I was letting my past dictate my future. *"This is what I've always done"* was looping in my mind and so was, *"This is what clients expect from me."* It wasn't until I gave myself permission to step outside the confines of my own expectations box that I could build a more satisfying vocation.

Ultimately, I asked myself, *"If I didn't keep doing what I've always done, what would I do instead?"* While it seems simple, the freedom inherent in that question allowed me to create new signature programs that became the basis for my consulting work. My income skyrocketed, and so did my enjoyment of life and work.

Blasting away my self-imposed parameters also led me to write this book and encouraged me to expand from simply providing business advice to creating content in the personal development genre. The best part is that adding the Resiliency Ninja movement to my message, inspired me to love my original work again. I think it's the combination of having a variety of topics and seeing the value of the business topics through a new lens – to solve obstacles and be resilient, you need to fix your revenue. I often get hired to do both the biz and the resilience messages at conferences because clients recognize how they are intertwined.

When you leave the past behind, it's important to make responsible decisions. Therefore, the next question I asked was, "How can I transition responsibly into my new vision?" There were a few things that helped. For example, I recorded my entire "Profitable Networking" training program and posted it online for purchase. Often clients will bring me in for the larger Infinite Sales Sequencing training I do, and then augment that with my online program. It works out even better for the client because they can access the training on their own schedule and repeat the learning opportunities anytime they like.

In the end, venturing outside my comfort zone proved to be worthwhile, profitable and fulfilling. When I first began to feel uninspired by my topic, I didn't have the confidence or self-awareness to explore other options. I just kept wallowing, looping back to the same issue instead of taking a leap in a new direction.

I spent several years putting Band-Aids on my business, like a new logo, revamped website or snazzier titles on presentations. None of those solutions had the depth to truly reignite my joy for business. Who knows where my business might be today if I had grabbed the rope sooner.

Staying stuck in the past or using old reference points to define your future can blind you to the great resources around you. Do you say, "Yeah, but" every time a good idea comes around, or resist a helpful hand because of preconceived notions about how this will play out, skewed by past experiences?

The past can only rob you of your future if you give it the power to do so. Soaking in bitterness and resentment regarding the hellish moments of the past is like manufacturing your own quicksand pit and diving into it head-first.

It's up to you to acknowledge earlier experiences, thank them for the lessons learned, and move forward to the future with new knowledge and an open mind. Otherwise, you'll stay stuck.

The most successful entrepreneurs I know won't enable anyone in their path to stay stuck. Their entire essence is moving forward and finding solutions. Many practice a "two-loop limit." That means they won't listen to the same problem more than twice. The first time they let you share and perhaps complain a little; the second time they expect to be hearing about solutions. They don't want to hear about the same subject a third time because they consider it whining – which means you're wasting their time.

It may sound harsh, but think about the number of times you've spent months or even years enabling a friend (or yourself) to keep looping the same story about an old partner, a lost promotion, a failed speech or a bullying boss? Maybe allotting just two conversations to discuss and solve a problem is too few for you; it was for me. But there needs to be an expectation that at some point, sooner rather than later, you're going to take action to move forward instead of wallowing in the same circumstance. Taking baby steps to progress in the right direction is better than complaining about the same thing over and over, sinking in quicksand.

One sure-fire way to stay stuck is to try to figure out why bad things happen. Unfortunately, there may never be a deep reason that will bring you the comfort you seek. It's hard to accept hard knocks when we don't understand why they're happening. If you have been returning again and again to the same issue hoping to find an answer, you must learn to accept that you may never know why. You'll need to find peace with that. One way I do this is to create a reason that comforts me. I may not be right, but at least this allows me to resolve an issue and move on.

Resiliency Ninja Formula

Self-Awareness +

Strength (♡ Heart + Mental + Physical) +

Resourcefulness = Resiliency Ninja

 Are you stuck in toxic patterns and ignoring the solutions that are all around you?

 Do you say, "Yeah, but" when ideas and solutions are presented to you?

 From a feeling of freedom, ask yourself, "If I didn't keep doing what I've always done, what would I do instead?"

 The past does not have the authority to rob you of your future unless you give it the power to do so.

 You may never know why something bad happened, so stop looping and trying to guess answers. Create a reason that comforts you and allows you to get unstuck.

12

You Can't Fake Forgiveness

I WISH I COULD FORGIVE like Winston does. When I get back from a trip he is elated. After I pick him up and he's offered a few frantic kisses, he realizes that he's supposed to be angry with me for leaving him. It's adorable. While I'm holding him, he moves his head away from me, as if to say, "I'm not talking to you right now. No more kisses for you." A minute later he's already over it and back to being overjoyed.

If only humans could forgive so easily.

My Dad was like that in many ways. He would get irritated, express a firm opinion and five minutes later he'd be totally over it.

For day-to-day annoyances, I'm the same as dad. It's hard to get me riled for long. Unfortunately, when the worst happens, like true adversities or breaches of trust, the five-minute "forgive and forget" approach stops working. Despite pretending it did, I learned the hard way that minimizing their impact or just brushing off the most difficult life experiences is not the answer to a joyful existence.

Deflecting is essentially faking forgiveness, which doesn't serve your long-term heart healing.

Initially I thought I was quick to forgive because I would just deflect and ignore a problem or diminish its existence. Dr. T called it my "Gotta Go" technique. When I didn't like what was happening over "here" I'd just go over "there." The problem with this approach is that eventually there was nowhere left to go—and I found myself surrounded by the emotions I had refused to process earlier.

Through everything, forgiveness has been the hardest part of my journey. True forgiveness takes grace, understanding and determination, and at times I just didn't have any of those qualities.

Finally, I realized that forgiveness happens in an instant, but the processing that leads to the moment of letting go takes its own time.

For a long while, I had no intention of ever forgiving the surgeon who botched my surgery. I was 100 percent committed to hating him for the rest of my life.

I resented that he wasn't a better surgeon, that he caused me so much pain and that he didn't take responsibility for his actions. I hated that he robbed me of my prime time to have kids and he turned my life upside down. I hated that he had the nerve to write a line in my file about me that sets the feminist movement back to the dark ages. (I won't even dignify it by repeating his comment.)

Every time I went to another doctor to try to fix his handiwork, I offered a little ode to that first surgeon, and it was definitely not a love poem. I hated that for the first couple of years I only saw doctors who had either trained him or trained with him. I hated the system and how certain cliques of doctors protect their own so that if they mess up in the future, a colleague won't testify against them.

I hated how some doctors dismissed my pain because I looked fine on the outside, wasn't moping, and hadn't given up on life. I resented that the hospital where I had the first surgery allowed a nurse to force me to drive home high-as-a-kite the next morning, shortly after another nurse had plied me with drugs. Even worse, I resented that when I made a complaint the administration blamed me and insisted I left on my own volition, which was not true, but even if it was true, it wasn't a valid excuse.

Then I hated myself for not taking pictures and recording every step of the journey. I hated knowing that had I fallen asleep after my second surgery when I went home with a nicked artery, I could have bled to death. I was also outraged that the surgeon who spent hours putting pressure on my bleeding artery while we waited for an operating room, wrote such a cursory mention of the artery cauterization in my file that the hospital and doctor could deny, once again, that they had messed up.

I also hated that when I filed a formal complaint about the botched surgery and subsequent debacles, I had to spend a full day in a room with merciless representatives from the College of Physicians and Surgeons who refused to understand the truth of what happened as the surgeon's lawyer twisted everything I said to blame me. Heck, I even resented that that lawyer ever became a lawyer and had the gall to defend a man who injured me so callously.

I could go on because, despite my smile, I was in a constant state of hate, anger and disappointment. I felt like I'd been punched—and then while I was on the ground the entire healthcare system delivered an even stronger kick, like a bully on the playground.

I felt like no one was on my side. Not the college of physicians, the body that is supposed to protect patients; not my lawyers; and not the two-faced doctors who said one thing in the examination room and wrote something different in my file. *"Holy crap, what did that doctor do to you?"* comes to mind as one example of what was said to me by an emergency room doctor, but her concern was never written down on my file.

Once I listened to three doctors talk about me within ear shot of the waiting room, and I felt violated all over again. I resented that the start of several medical memos included some version of *"she's a lovely, friendly young woman"* as if somehow, being pleasant negated my pain.

There were a hundred reasons why I held hate in my heart. Not one of them served my healing.

One night while I was lying in bed, I decided I'd had enough anger. Finally, I was ready to let it go. I signed release documents on my legal case that had been sitting on my desk for months, with the words *"Do better next time"* just above my signature.

How did I finally forgive and let go?

Here's my Resiliency Ninja Forgiveness Framework:
- Feel the full pain of the situation.
- Reposition the interpretation of the wrongdoers' intent.
- Build a story around the experience that will serve your healing.
- Recognize the blessings in the situation.
- Focus on the present and the future.

Feel the Full Pain: I don't believe we can really move forward until we've felt and acknowledged the full extent of the hurt. I'll tear up at a happy or sad commercial, or when I see someone doing a good deed, but to sit and expose myself to the worst, most devastating emotions in my heart, no thanks. Until I did I couldn't resolve the emotions, and forgiveness was impossible.

Diminish, distract and deflect were my avoidance techniques. As soon as I started to feel the hurt bubble up I would push it back down again by immersing myself in another activity. I couldn't handle the overwhelming agony of feeling the emotions that had become the background music in my life.

Now I realize that the key to letting go of hurts is to acknowledge them to the fullest extent possible for you. It's hard to sit in the stillness of agony, but the sooner you do, the faster the core of your negative emotions will dissipate permanently. In some extremely difficult circumstances, such as sexual assault, sitting in the full essence of the agony at once may be too overwhelming. Instead, I've found it helpful to accept and dissipate the pain in layers. One small step at a time.

It's like tensing every muscle in your body. When you let go, you immediately feel a wave of relaxation you could never have felt if you hadn't experienced the tension in its harshest form.

Try that now. Curl your toes and your calves and all the way up your legs. Then make a fist and tighten every arm muscle. Contract your belly and your glutes. Hold it, tight, tight, tight for a count of five and then let go. Completely relax. Let the blood rush through your body. Feel that sensation of relief? This is how you can heal your heart too.

In the thick of your pain it may take a while to heal. The old residual pain needs to come to the forefront and be felt, or you'll never truly be able to move forward.

As I started my forgiveness journey I had to relive and acknowledge every gut-wrenching emotion associated with my experience; without that, I could have never been able to let it all go. To some extent it would always be there, nagging my heart and holding me captive.

Journaling was a helpful way to organize my feelings. Seeing your feelings put down in writing can give you new perspectives. You may notice themes of shame or personal blame that you haven't processed yet.

During my forgiveness journey, I wrote some horrific, hateful prose. Eventually I burned the notes to release the anger into flames, but not until the full extent of my feelings had dissipated.

Interpreting Intent: Understanding the reason another person acted a certain way can change the bitterness in your heart. A lot of healing can be done by understanding a person's intent in any situation. As humans, we may fail in our delivery, but understanding that motivation was pure and good-natured makes it easier to forgive.

If someone intended to cause you harm, that's harder to forgive than an accident. For example, I must believe that my surgical nightmare was caused unintentionally. Perhaps incompetence played a factor, but I don't think my surgeon walked into the operating room planning to screw up a surgery.

Flipping to see the event through the other person's eyes can be difficult and takes patience. I spent a lot of time trying to see my surgeries through the doctor's eyes. It was the only way to shift my perception of what happened. I would walk through the scenario, imagining how he felt to be given a medical case simply because he was the doctor on call. I started to empathize with him because he has to live, and continue to perform risky operations, knowing that his hands caused a domino effect of hell in my life. I don't know if he actually cares, but I decided to believe he does. As a doctor his creed is "Do no harm," and while he did cause serious injury, I'm trusting it wasn't intentional.

I think you could say I was trying to empathize with him rather than focusing on the me-against-him loop I had imprinted in my mind.

That's unlike when someone attacks or sexually assaults another person. There is no explanation that makes those despicable acts right. Unfortunately, as a victim, the instinct is to own the intent. *"I deserved that, I should have protected myself. How could I let him do that to me?"* It's better to place the blame where it lies, solely on the perpetrator.

Build a Story to Serve Your Healing: In my early twenties, when I was selling cars before I became a receptionist, my boss always said, "A person's perception is his reality." It's that saying, repeated over and over in my mind, that made me recognize I needed to create a new narrative which would allow me to create a new, better-serving perception of reality for myself. Some may call it making justifications, but I just tried to see the story through a more supportive lens to change my perception of reality.

I'd say things like, *"With every surgical procedure there are risks, it's so like me to be the one in a million. There are worse things that could have happened, I must be thankful for small blessings. I'm strong enough to get through this and the universe is just testing my resolve. I'm going to be a Resiliency Ninja after this."*

Repeating these affirmations didn't erase my hurts, but it did allow me to soften the blow and promote healing. Anything I could do to flip the story to be less hateful and more accepting furthered my recovery and my quest to be a Resiliency Ninja

Recognize the Blessings: As much as I endured many bad experiences with doctors, I also met caring doctors who offered incredible support throughout my journey. They may not have written it down in their reports, but they put in the time to try to make up for the way the healthcare system had mistreated me. Some bent over backwards to help, empathizing and sympathizing while they spent hours on my case. Focusing on those glimmers of kindness and not the worst aspects of my story melted the hatred away and replaced it with love and appreciation.

It also helped to focus on the positive outcomes that came from the surgeries. I slowed down, learned better how to deal with my emotions, and became more self-aware. In the ensuing months, I created a business that paid me handsomely for part-time work, Mom moved to town, and I found Winston and brought him home. Constantly reminding yourself of the positive aspects of life that are often taken for granted can help speed your path to forgiveness.

Focus on the Future: Wallowing in the past keeps you stuck in the quicksand of trauma and pain. I used to get flashbacks replaying various aspects of my misfortunes all the time. They would send me spinning. I'd remember the second I woke up after the operation, the excruciating pain, and the nurse's reaction. He said you wouldn't believe what we took out of you, and then brought me a jar to show me. Was his enthusiasm really necessary? But replaying those moments never helped. Instead, when these incidents flashed into my mind, I would acknowledge the memory, thank it for reminding me to cherish today's better, less traumatic moments, and shift my thinking back to the present. I had to make a conscious decision to remove myself from the horrors of the operating room and focus on where I was. I had to start appreciating that I was not dwelling in that past any longer.

Acknowledging a bad memory's presence and purpose, rather than trying to pretend it doesn't exist, slowly lessened the frequency of my flashbacks and reduced their intensity.

The imagination is a powerful tool. It can take us back in time and make us relive old horrors all over again. Replacing those sensations with new, healthier feelings was a major step that helped me let go.

This framework works in all types of situations that require forgiveness. Sometimes the hardest person to forgive is yourself. Accept that you did the best you could with the knowledge and emotional intelligence you had at the time. Now you know better and you can draw on your new insights whenever similar situations arise in the future.

Until you've achieved authentic forgiveness from the bottom of your heart, it won't be possible to heal completely from your worst, most excruciating experiences.

Resiliency Ninja Formula

Self-Awareness +

Strength (Heart + Mental + Physical) +

Resourcefulness = Resiliency Ninja

♡ *There could be a hundred reasons why you have hate in your heart, but not one of them will serve your healing.*

♡ *Forgiveness happens in an instant, but the processing that leads to the true moment of letting go takes time.*

♡ *Most importantly, forgive yourself. You did the best you could with the knowledge and resources you had at the time.*

♡ *The Resiliency Ninja's Forgiveness Framework:*
  - *Feel the full pain.*
  - *Reposition the interpretation of the wrongdoer's intent.*
  - *Build a story around the experience that will serve your healing.*
  - *Recognize the blessings in the situation.*
  - *Focus on the present and the future.*

Humans may fail in delivery, but understanding that their motivation was pure and good-natured can make forgiveness easier.

13

The Internal Messenger of BS

THE MIND PLAYS TRICKS. When you have only a tiny bit of information around a topic or event, combining that nugget of truth with an active imagination can make for some wildly adventuresome scenarios in our minds that have only a passing resemblance to reality.

Our brains want to fill in the missing details in a story. And goodness knows, we rarely fill in those blanks with positive messages. Instead, we tend to add fearful details that provide maximum support for worrying and judgment. Repeatedly, people jump to imaginary conclusions that aren't only wrong, but self-destructive.

No one knows the number of thoughts we have each day. But there are many statistics that say 50 to 80 percent of all of our thoughts are negative ones. I believe it.

It's time to bring these negative internal conversations to light and turn them inside out. Be kinder to yourself and start to interpret your surroundings in the best possible light.

One of my clients is very task-oriented. When he's on a mission to get something done, or dealing with a problem, he can walk through the hallways of his office building in complete silence, oblivious to the number of people he's ignoring. Once he's dealt with those nagging details, he'll walk through the same halls smiling, laughing and saying hello to everyone he meets. It's just how he is.

Quite routinely, however, his team members will confide in me that they think he hates them and they're afraid they're going to lose their jobs. The source of their fears: he walked through the halls and didn't notice or acknowledge them. Whoa! Here is the internal messenger of bullshit, filling in blanks with elaborate, inaccurate stories. Once I explained that his behavior stems from his stress and personality type, and has nothing to do with them, they relaxed and rewrote the story in their heads to eliminate the destructive fable they were creating out of nothing.

You've probably experienced similar dire situations, invented either by you or by someone you know. Some examples:

So and so called and left me a message to call her, something must be wrong. No, you don't know that yet; maybe she just wants to say hi.

Why didn't you call me when you got to the hotel? I thought maybe you were in an accident. If I was, I trust the police would have called you. I got hungry, dropped off my bags and went to the restaurant right away.

She didn't say hi, she must be angry with me. Actually no, she just didn't see you, because she was focused on something else.

Each of us is locked in our own perception of reality, which in turn is influenced most by the voices in our heads. When the proverbial fan powers on high, this internal voice and the story it makes up out of tiny shreds of information can either reduce our stress or aggravate the problems we face.

The good news is that each of us gets to choose if we'll build our storylines from a pessimistic or optimistic point of view. For example, a friend once told me that when he hears an ambulance racing down the street, he chooses to believe that a baby is being born, rather than imagining the tragedies that often precede a blaring siren.

Your internal voice can become very loud and destructive, unless you tame it and then train it to be a helpful partner on your life's journey. You may sometimes think you're the only one with a harsh inner critic, but you're not. We all have one.

When we're dealing with invisible adversities, the stuff outsiders can't see, your inner critic can make you feel caged in your own private hell. The worst circumstances can inspire the worst stories.

More times than I'd like to admit, I felt alone in my suffering while assuming that everyone else was just skating happily through life. The internal messenger of bullshit manufactured the story that I was some sort of unfortunate anomaly. The truth is that no one is spared; I see that now.

Although, as a sidebar, one friend recently told me she has never heard from her negative inner critic. I wanted to poke her to see if she's real. I had to warn her: "As a heads-up, you may not understand my book."

No matter how frustrated you may be feeling right now, please, realize that you are not alone. There is comfort when we know that other people have survived and overcome similar circumstances. Unfortunately, we don't normally get a glimpse of others' struggles until after the fact, if ever.

Watching others succeed, while being oblivious to their inner struggles, feeds our instinct to engage in unfair and inaccurate comparisons, where misery finds its most comfortable resting place.

A misbehaving inner voice amplifies challenging forces from outside. It's like having a messenger walking beside you every day shouting shitty things at you. You're ugly, you're dumb, they are so much better than you, you shouldn't even bother trying. How can you adapt and be resilient during life's suckiest moments if this messenger is your constant companion and it's an asshole?

That's why I'm on a mission to calm this unwelcome intruder. I hope you will commit to train your inner voice to think from a kinder perspective that will enhance your success rather than sabotage it.

Healing from wounds and finding your authentic path is a process: you'll have good days and bad days. The goal is to find new strength that makes it possible to charge right through your troubles and have inner peace while you do. The stories you tell yourself about what's happening will determine how easily you can achieve your desired outcome.

Resiliency Ninjas see their internal messenger of BS for exactly what it is: a traitor to the cause, a harbinger of despair and a precursor to defeat. They trust the real facts, not fears, to lead them through difficult times. Your solution may not be obvious in the moment, but when you calm the internal messenger of BS, it will be easier for you to find your path to success no matter what challenges blow your way.

Resiliency Ninja Formula

Self-Awareness +

Strength (Heart + Mental + Physical) +

Resourcefulness = Resiliency Ninja

 Your perception of reality is most influenced by the voice inside your head that will either aggravate or reduce difficult situations.

 In the absence of factual information, your imagination will fill in the blanks to craft a story. It's up to you to be sure that supporting information serves your mental well-being.

 The internal voice can become very destructive unless you first tame it then train it to be a helpful participant on your life's journey. Make peace with it, it's your constant companion for your whole life.

 Bring your internal messenger of B.S. to the forefront by writing down the non-factual stories you're adding around negative situations. Write two alternative stories with more positive narratives for the same circumstance and see if that changes your perspective.

14

Turning Sticks into Sinkholes

THERE'S A BIG DIFFERENCE BETWEEN obstacles, true adversity and everyday stress that most people face. Each of these challenges resides on a sliding scale of hurt and frustration, which require varied approaches to overcome. Throughout our life, each of us will face stress, obstacles and adversity, and being self-aware enough to recognize which level of challenge you are facing in a given moment will be your cue to use the right tool at the right time.

Synonyms for *stress* include pressure, tension, worry, anxiety, hassle, demands and strain.

Synonyms for *obstacle* are barrier, hurdle, block, snag, deterrent, disadvantage, hindrance and complication.

Synonyms for *adversity* include misfortune, hardship, disaster, suffering, misery, trauma, accident, crisis, catastrophe and burden.

See the difference?

The catalyst for each is varied. Stress is largely driven by your internal interpretation of outside influences. Obstacles are actual barriers in your path. You have the power to choose whether to conquer them or simply bypass them. True adversity is a negative, often tragic, external force that's completely out of your control. The only aspects of adversity that you can influence are your perspective and recovery.

Imagine you're walking along a path in the woods.

An example of stress in this scenario would occur if it started to rain heavily while you're walking causing you to return home early without achieving your distance goal. You may be disappointed, or even soaking wet, but your world is not crumbling. This may annoy you, and if you don't separate the emotion from the failed goal, will cause you unnecessary stress.

Let's say you come upon a stick blocking your feet. Is it an obstacle on your path? Sure. Is it adversity? Nope. In fact, Winston would just pick it up and start chewing it like a tasty snack. Sometimes people treat little sticks like thick logs, towering cliffs or raging floods, when they're really mere sticks you can pick up and move out of the way.

As you're walking along the path, an example of adversity might be an earthquake that collapses the ground in front of you, causing a dangerous sinkhole that's impossible to cross. Your world has changed, and you need to make major adjustments like building a bridge over the sinkhole before continuing your hike. When true adversity strikes it's important to prioritize time for healing and responding appropriately, as we'll discuss in Chapter 16: *The Toughest Stuff*.

In the real world, stress is a result of unrealistic expectations you place on yourself. It is rarely caused by a specific task; it occurs because you choose not to control your schedule effectively and you try to do too much in too little time. It's easy to get overwhelmed. There is always more to do. What causes undue stress is the unrealistic assumption that your to-do list will eventually end. A to-do list is never finished; in fact, I call it a to-do circle because it just keeps going around and around. In truth, while you may believe that everything on your list *must* be done, much of it could be delegated, ignored or tackled in more manageable ways.

Learning how to master your time and become more discerning about what you allow into your to-do circle will free you from unnecessary stress. In future chapters, you'll learn how to effectively achieve your top priorities without feeling like you're paddling a kayak upstream against hurricane-induced waves.

Exaggerating our stresses and obstacles is common. It's easy to get stuck on a small issue until you've created an entire dramatic story around it. Once you 'mountainize' an anthill, your mind thinks the stress and obstacles are giant adversities. It's much harder to power through or find solutions when you're interpreting reasonably negative circumstances as tragic events. Overstating the power of your opposition is another behavior that puts unnecessary strain on your resiliency muscles.

An obstacle in life is annoying and often causes frustration, but there is always a way to move it, go through it, ignore it or blow it up. The longer you take to address the obstacle and find a solution, the bigger the obstacle will seem. Looking at obstacles objectively allows you to see the stick for what it is – a minor impediment in your path. If you can't master overcoming obstacles quickly and by using the right tools, then they can create an unmanageable swarm of problems, that collectively turn reasonable obstacles into what appear to be major adversities.

Adversity might involve being taken by fraudsters, having to declare bankruptcy, getting a diagnosis of terminal cancer, or losing someone you love. These sorts of hellish experiences require a stronger set of tools to get you out of bed each day.

You'll deal with stress, obstacles and adversity at different points in your life. You may even deal regularly with all three, leaving you feeling as if the tormenting trifecta will never end. Hoping all these setbacks will stop is not a strategy; it's a sure-fire way to make it harder to rebound from nasty situations.

A good start for becoming a Resiliency Ninja is to stop the habit of turning the sticks on your path into sinkholes. Placing each of your challenges in the appropriate spot on your sliding scale allows you to bring out the right tools at the right time to deal with each.

To clarify what you're facing, make a list of all your troubles so you can determine the severity of each. Go through your list and objectively classify each problem as either a stress, an obstacle, an adversity, or a non-issue that can safely be ignored. You'll likely have a mixture of all four. Naming them will help you prioritize your energy and figure out how to solve or work around the issues at hand. We'll explore this concept more fully in Chapter 34: *Expect Miracles, Strategize Solutions*. Until then, having a comprehensive list of challenges you face and determining their correct status are good self-awareness exercises to help you objectively manage the chaos and build resilience.

Resiliency Ninja Formula

Self-Awareness +

Strength (♡ Heart + Mental + Physical) +

Resourcefulness = Resiliency Ninja

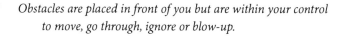

 Non-issues are exactly that ... non-issues. Decide now to not waste your energy and time trying to deal with them. Let them work themselves out. Most importantly, stop building negative storylines around them.

 Stress is driven from the internal interpretation of outside influences and is often the result of unrealistic expectations.

Obstacles are placed in front of you but are within your control to move, go through, ignore or blow-up.

Adversity is a negative, often tragic, external force that is out of your control. You can only influence your reaction to it and your strategies to heal.

The amplification of stress and obstacles into adversity strains your resiliency muscle. Do you tend to treat daily stress as obstacles or adversities? If so this makes it harder to become a Resiliency Ninja.

 A to-do list never ends, so I call it a to-do circle. Accepting the never-ending flow of tasks takes away pressure and unrealistic expectations to complete everything.

 Make a list of all the challenges flying at you. Categorize each as a stress, obstacle or adversity to put the gravity of each situation into perspective and help you plan your strategy to minimize their impact on you.

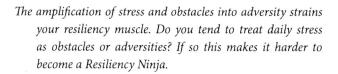

15

The Ice Cube that Became a Snowman

ANOTHER WAY TO THINK OF life's pains and how the interpretation of reality can be negatively exaggerated is to imagine an ice cube at the top of a huge hill which is covered with freshly fallen snow. The ice cube is your stress or obstacle. Push the ice cube into the fresh snow and it will collect a layer of snow all around it. Now you've got a snowball, with a problem frozen inside. If you give the ice cube a push down the hillside it will keep rolling and pick up more snow along the way, just like in a cartoon. By the time your snow-covered ice cube reaches the foot of the hill, it will be large enough to be the bottom of a snowman.

Your problems are represented by the ice cube. The drama a person manufactures around those issues by the internal messenger of B.S. and thanks to a lack of emotional intelligence, are the packing snow that attaches to the ice cube. Do you think it's easier to deal with an ice cube or with an entire snow boulder of doom?

Many people deal with difficulties in this manner. Objectively, the problem is just an ice cube and yet, because they obsess over it and exaggerate the optics around it, it turns into an abominable snowball. When you're in the thick of an issue, these habits can blindside you and make fixable problems feel insurmountable. The more defeatist the stories that collect around an issue, the more intense the pain will be – physically and emotionally.

The stories you tell yourself and the questions you ask around any situation will either magnify or minimize a problem and its impact. It's up to you to decide if you are a victim or a victor. Had I listened to the doctors and other pain patients and not chosen the path of the Resiliency Ninja, I would be out of business, living on disability and most likely miserable.

Instead, thanks to deciding to not let my life's challenges define my level of success, I am thankful to be living my dream speaking to audiences, writing books and serving others. It's not about minimizing negative situations; it's about seeing them exactly as they are. Magnifying and dramatizing stressful circumstances and obstacles makes it harder to break free and overcome. It also disrespects the need to honor and heal from our true adversities.

In my pain support group, I was sitting with a bunch of people who had turned their pain into snowmen. Many were 100 percent covered in packed snow. Based on the stories I heard in that room, they had no intention of breaking free. In a group dynamic, when one person has a victim mentality and is a master at packing snow around the ice cubes in the room, others are vulnerable to think and feel the same way. The loudest voice in any group dictates the vibe. That's why who you're interacting with daily and what information you feed your mind is so important. Unfortunately, a very strong victim of circumstances led the vibe of my group. As the new person, I soon realized I wouldn't genuinely be welcome until they had sucked all the remaining spirit of hope out of me. While they were trying to sell me this tale of doom and gloom with its exaggerated statements of life long impact which I should embrace as a pain patient, I was sitting there wondering "What's with this f#@&ing ice cube and how do I melt it?"

Big difference.

Refusing the victim path doesn't make me special; it's a choice every one of us needs to make in the face of any challenge.

Think of that metaphoric fan blowing in your face. Is it easier to keep moving forward if there are little specs of dust coming at you or huge chunks of asphalt? When you strip away the story and all its exaggerations you are in a better position to control your outcomes, despite what challenges are flying at you.

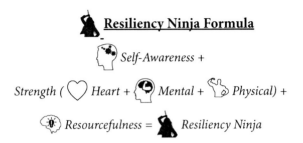

Resiliency Ninja Formula

Self-Awareness +

Strength (♡ Heart + Mental + Physical) +

Resourcefulness = Resiliency Ninja

 What drama are you adding to your difficult circumstances that make it harder to be a Resiliency Ninja?

 See your issues for exactly what they are rather than turning an ice cube into a snowman.

 Are you choosing to be a victim or a victor?

Review your list of challenges from earlier. Write the facts of each story, then decipher what's the drama you've added to them that can lead you to feeling like a victim.

16

The Toughest Stuff

AFTER DAD WAS DIAGNOSED WITH cancer, I noticed the gradual changes in the color of his skin, the vitality in his eyes and the meat on his bones. It was hard to watch. My brother and I spent a year and a half shuttling back and forth to our childhood home to help Mom care for Dad. She never left his side; it was an incredible example of love. Living over an hour away, there was an anxiety every time the phone rang that this could be 'the' call. The constant worrying that death is imminent creates an always-on-edge existence that makes it hard to focus on work.

A common theme in the severe-illness journey is that most people want to pretend that everything is going to be okay. Those gathered around try to save face. "You're going to bounce back," they say, knowing deep down that this person's time on earth is coming to an end. I remember feeling there was this elephant in the room no one wanted to acknowledge. I felt that we didn't let Dad speak freely, without interruption, about what was happening to his body and the prospect of death. Everyone wanted to stay positive, but looking back, I think talking about it would have made the grieving process easier. I wish we had talked more about his fears or acceptance of dying. I wish I knew what he wanted for us for the future and that he didn't feel cut-off whenever he tried to discuss "the end." I don't know for certain if he felt that frustration, but I certainly did.

It's hard to look head-on at the biggest adversities life has to offer and talk about the most devastating outcomes and the finality of death. Sure, when we feel vigorous and healthy we can talk about it more easily. But when humans are facing mortality in the eye, it is much harder to be strong and have the conversations that are needed most.

Why do we feel we need to be so strong? The dying patients may be wishing we would break down so that they can break down too. There is comfort in our vulnerabilities and if we don't acknowledge them they will follow us like a dark cloud everywhere we go.

How long does it take to go through the worst, most horrifying grief? Only you know what it takes for you. Go easy on your self-judgments, and slowly, but surely, you'll start to feel more like yourself, albeit a different version of yourself. I wish there was a magic answer that can erase the hurt.

By practicing the foundational thinking and tactics shared throughout this book, you'll be stronger when the worst happens. This will allow you to move forward faster. In my experience, the grieving process includes flashes of the superhero pose followed by random collapses to the fetal position. Accept the highs and lows and embrace the process from a supportive perspective.

When you truly are facing a sinkhole, you need to retreat and take care of yourself. Everything needs to be focused on what you need to do to best support your healing. If you don't honor the time you need to grieve or recover then you will be showing up for life only half-way, instead of waiting until you are ready to show up fully.

Time is the only true healer. Unfortunately, during the worst moments, it may feel like it's taking forever. It's easy to believe the devastation will never pass. It will, you'll get your spark back that is currently dimmed, but in truth, time only makes it easier to deal with the suckage. The ground that fell into the bottom of a sinkhole doesn't come back to the surface. It's gone forever. Sadly, time doesn't change that fact.

Adding to the burden of the toughest stuff is the natural tendency to long for a return to life before the loss. In upcoming pages, I'll share the importance of identifying what you can and cannot control. Time travel is not on the list of controllable aspects of adversity.

Crafting a new vision for your future is difficult when you are also being compelled to think of a future without the person or circumstance you're grieving. Be patient: new visions take time to achieve.

Aside from being kind to yourself and allowing yourself to go through the toughest stuff without judgments, I believe the key to getting through those worst times is to surround yourself with loyal loved ones who cushion you from the hardships of the world. Keep them around you to lean on while you're grieving, to support you while you're adjusting, and to welcome you back to the everyday world when you're ready to get back to it.

Two weeks before my 30th birthday, Dad died. Mom was devastated – and exhausted.

I remember giving her books about grieving to help her snap out of her despair. As if a book would suddenly make her forget 33 years of marriage. Looking back, I can see how insensitive it was for me to expect her to bounce back to her former, joyful self before she was ready.

It was like losing a parent all over again. I couldn't motivate her to start living a full life as a widow; she needed to experience the stages of grief in her own time.

There were many judgmental family members and friends who thought she should have bounced back faster, but they hadn't lost their spouse, and couldn't relate to the difficulty of imagining a future without her husband and best friend.

There were also many people who, now that she was a widow, didn't know what to say to her, so they just said nothing. I've talked with several widows who had the same experience. People want to respect the survivor's need for space and want to avoid tears, so they end up abandoning their friends after the hustle and bustle of the funeral. I remember Mom feeling completely bewildered and devastated when she would hear about the same group of couples getting together, as they had done for decades, only now she was no longer included. These exclusions not only gave my mom another kind of loss to grieve, but they also reduced her self-esteem and confidence at a crucial time when she needed them to be at their utmost.

For Mom, eventually the laughs returned, and she created a life that embraced her new normal, which is a term used to describe life after significant loss. The essence of this wording is that you can't return to your pre-loss level of happiness. You will always feel different, like something is missing, but you learn to live with it – you have no choice. As Dad used to say, "Life goes on".

In the second chapter, I mentioned that one of the biggest misconceptions about resiliency is that every day needs to be a good day. That's just not possible, especially when you're dealing with the toughest stuff.

Another common misconception perpetuated by the self-help industry is that with some positive thinking, every day can be all roses all the time. I disagree. When bad stuff happens, a Resiliency Ninja learns to recognize it, embrace it and thoughtfully deals with it. Wishing it away or making positive affirmations pretending the bad stuff doesn't exist is being näive. I do believe that having an optimistic outlook in a bad circumstance is highly valuable and makes it easier for you to adapt when your life falls apart.

So, when you encounter stress and obstacles, absolutely, power through, find your workarounds and keep your eye on the prize. For adversity, take a kinder approach. Acknowledge your feelings, find solutions to the immediate challenges you face, and prioritize time to let yourself grieve. Without that devotion to healing, it will take much longer to find a joyful path for your life.

Resiliency Ninja Formula

Self-Awareness +

Strength (Heart + Mental + Physical) +

Resourcefulness = Resiliency Ninja

 There is a time to power through and there is a time to honor your need to collapse in the fetal position – and to do so without judgment.

 There is no specific time to heal from grief or severe traumas. The more you honor your healing the faster you will move forward to a newer version of yourself.

 Wishing for the way things were will not serve your healing. It's about creating a new way of life that is acceptable.

17

The Greener Grass is Fake

LATELY I'VE BEEN HAVING SOME raw, authentic conversations with friends and colleagues about the gap between where we thought we should be by this point in our lives and the reality of where we are. These conversations have helped me realize that most of us, to some degree, are feeling disappointed with our life's progress.

Throw into that mix a number of periodic setbacks and life events that test you to your very core, then sprinkle those challenges with unrealistic expectations of how much you can accomplish in a day. The result: many people are walking around smiling on the outside, but inside feeling like failures, questioning their self-worth, fearing for their future and squashing their true potential.

The great internal divide is this gap between the perception of "should" and "reality." It lies at the root of unhappiness, frustration, lack of self-confidence and self-sabotage.

The wider that gap, the worse its impact.

While I admire people with a tiny gap, this book is for the rest of us.

Living with Mom for my thirties and dressing my dog in cute snowsuits was not how I envisioned my life. Having to smile through horrible pain and grief wasn't easy to accept, either. My thirties were supposed to be when I created a picturesque life with Mr. Right, 2.5 kids and a white picket fence. I expected a multiple-seven-figure speaking business, to be traveling the world in first class and to still fit into my favorite size-eight outfits.

So far, I have a fence….and it's not white.

"Should have" notions glisten in our minds like lawns of brilliantly green grass on the other side of the fence. It's easy to pine for the idealized fairy tale, but they are just figments of imagination you encounter when you compare your goals – usually unfairly – against your current reality. If the grass on the other side looks greener, that's because it is probably fake.

"If only I had" and "shoulda, woulda, coulda" start way too many conversations that end up leaving us with a feeling that, compared to almost everyone else, we're not good enough. These feelings of inadequacy make boomeranging even more challenging.

Continual growth is a universal need. As humans, if we had everything we ever dreamed of we would become stagnant, there would be nothing left to motivate us to do better.

There is a big difference between striving toward personally-inspired goals, which is healthy, rather than judging oneself for being lightyears away from unrealistic fantasies of what life should really be like.

Where do these unattainable expectations come from? Family, peers, and personal experiences surely influence our desires and our judgments, but I think we could manage expectations more easily if it were just our inner circle guiding us. Instead, I believe society as a whole does the most to make us aim for perfection and see our current accomplishments as "less than." Society pressures us to live some idealized perception of "exceptional normal," and then we chastise ourselves for not achieving this ridiculous standard.

It's an advertiser's job to broaden the divide between your ideal expectations and your perceived reality. Savvy marketers remind us how far our reality has drifted from our ideal futures, before kindly pointing out that their product or service is the magic answer that will close the gap. So, we buy that solution and feel happy for a moment, until we realize we've been had and buy the next shiny, blinky thing that catches our eye.

There's another reason that we are constantly feeling that life should be better. It's because we deny, or forget, that the mechanics of life are usually fairly mundane, with peaks of enthusiastic greatness. We all want more of the fun stuff, less of the boring.

When we see our friends, family members or movie stars celebrate their successful moments on social media we internalize this myth that every online snapshot is a true reflection of someone's real world. Why do we judge ourselves based on others' picture-perfect moments in time? It teases us with implausible notions that everyone else is having all the fun, as if there's a secret formula for greatness that only we somehow missed. Meanwhile, others are looking at your online posts and thinking, "Wow, do you ever have it together."

See, there's just no winning with comparisons.

Speaking of perfect-picture moments, is there a more idealized image than that of the Royal Family, specifically the love story of William and Kate and their children? I have never seen a bad picture of Kate. It's uncanny. When the couple got engaged I was in awe. "Wow, lucky her, she got her prince." Mom responded to me the same way her dad spoke to her when they watched the 1953 Coronation ceremony in which Princess Elizabeth became Queen. Like so many children watching that seemingly magical event, my mom was wishing she was a royal princess.

Just as Grampa told mom, she told me, "Be thankful for your life for you don't know the challenges others face. Imagine never getting to go where you want, when you want with the privacy you want. You have the privilege to do and be anything, whereas many of her life's decisions will be made for her."

For as perfect and put together as the Duchess of Cambridge is, with all due respect, I can't imagine that her kids don't have temper tantrums and smelly diapers, or a fear of thunderstorms. They are all just humans. Sure, they're humans with staff, money and privilege, but none of that can protect you from life's pain.

So how do you narrow the gap between should and reality? What I found helpful was to better align my "should" with my perceived reality. Alignment is achieved by challenging and rewriting the "shoulds" that haunt you; then more accurately assess your current state. Closing the internal divide makes it easier to handle whatever life throws at you.

There are several ways to do this.

For starters, become intentional about monitoring your expectations. In what ways is the "should-vs.-reality" conflict causing you frustration? Write down your failed expectations for your life and any lingering "shoulds."

Replace your "should" stories with new "I want" expectations. This restores hope for the future because the "shoulds" in life rarely get done. "Should" is a defeatist word.

"*I should write a book.*" If you want to write, get writing. If the idea of all the writing, editing and tweaking gives you hives (I assure you it takes a lot of effort.) then really ask yourself why you think you should do that. Not everyone has to write a book. I believe everyone has a book inside them, but that doesn't mean it's going to get written. Maybe sharing your message through video or audio is a better option for you. Maybe there are better ways to contribute to the world without becoming publicly vulnerable by telling your story.

"*I should expand by business to new territories.*" Why? Will expansion really grow your income, or just add to your headaches, travel time and expense line?

"I should get a new job." Really? What will be different if you work somewhere else? Will you leave your internal dissatisfaction behind? Most likely the issues you face at one job will follow you to the next until you learn to solve your internal problems.

Who or what is feeding these "shoulds" in your life? Are they showing up as regrets?

Regret is basically the "shoulds" of the past. The "I should have done X" syndrome will drive you bonkers because you can't go back in time. Wallowing in missed opportunities in the past clogs your brain's power to shape your future in a positive light.

If your "shoulds" are all in the past tense, ask yourself if there is any way you can still achieve "X" or even a reasonable substitute. Yes? Then go for it. No? Then write a new storyline that makes you feel better by eliminating regrets you can't change.

I remember my dad always regretted not accepting an invitation to buy a promising fast-food franchise when my older brother was born. Instead, he moved the family to his home town area to start a small-town life. Sure, he could argue that that $30,000 franchise is today worth a million or more, but does that make his decision wrong? All the blessings that came from having his children grow up on a lake surrounded by family and friends have far outweighed the potential money he missed.

A big problem with regret is that you really don't know if you would be happier if you had taken some other path. Maybe you'd still have the same challenges set against a slightly different set of circumstances, and maybe you'd be miserable. It's easy to idealize the path not taken.

Dr. T. and I have debated this. If I hadn't had the surgery, would I have ever learned to slow down and appreciate the roses? Would I have run for politics? Would I have written my first, second and now my third book? Would I have had such a great relationship with my mom? Would I have ever found Winston? Would I still have met all my incredible new friends if it weren't for my hardships?

I argue that none of these blessings would have been possible, because the botched surgery was the first domino to fall which sent me on a path that eventually brought all the above into my life. Dr. T. disagrees. He says each person has the power to choose and if those instincts and accomplishments spring from within, then they would eventually have happened anyway, possibly with different catalysts. Perhaps I would have written different books or run for political office later in my life, as I originally planned. It's impossible to say.

Once you choose a path you need to be confident you've made the best decision with the information and resources you had. Living in the past and rehashing old decisions drains precious mental energy you need today. Commit to rewriting your regrets so you can enjoy the present and shape your future path without the heavy baggage of yesterday.

Never let regrets from the past or desires for the future negate your satisfaction of today.

I think age plays a large part in broadening the internal divide between "should" and reality. It's true we can't turn back time. We get to a certain age and we think we should be further ahead by that stage. There is no way to change the past, so instead we have to protect the future from regrets. Be grateful to be on the right side of the grass, commit to honoring your remaining days, and reject regret by better aligning your wants and outcomes.

I do believe that if you should miss an opportunity that was meant to be on your life's path, then a similar chance will present itself again. Next time you'll be more prepared and better equipped to make decisions you won't regret.

Since the great internal divide is the gap between expectations and perceived reality, and we now agree that most of your "shoulds" are unrealistic, hollow baggage, then it's safe to assume that your perception of your current achievements may be misaligned as well.

The gap between should and reality is magnified when we interpret our current reality as worse than it really is. Celebrating wins in the moment is difficult because you're always benchmarking your accomplishments against those unrealistic expectations. It's an unending circle of frustration.

I've had an ongoing struggle with my body image. There's been a huge gap between my "shoulds" and my perception of my reality. When I was a size eight I took it for granted and longed instead to be a size four or six. (FYI, the last time a lady's size four fit over my thighs was the summer before grade six.) I spent most of my teens, 20s and early 30s believing that fluctuating between a size eight and twelve qualified me as "fat". OMG, if I could only be as "fat" as I thought I was back then.

In grade six I became so obsessed with squeezing back into my smaller clothes from the year before that I ended up with an eating disorder through high school – ultimately culminating in a hospital stay during university. Eating disorders are about much more than body weight, so I don't want to make light of the problem. I believe that the root of most eating disorders lies in a self-loathing that stems from this great internal competition that we've been talking about in this chapter.

Focusing solely on my body-weight issue and not my eating disorder, because it deserves the respect of a larger conversation, you can see that my "should" was unrealistic for my body. My perception of reality was all askew, making me believe I was fat when I was trim and healthy back then. That perception-compared-to-reality gap caused much unhappiness over the years. Then, not so shockingly, my body expanded to meet my mental image of the shape I thought I was.

On the good news front, I have accepted my fluctuating body size these days thanks to Winston's inspiration. His unconditional love applies no matter if I'm a 10 or an 18. His lack of interest in my weight made me realize how little love is influenced by people's shapes and sizes. From a health perspective, of course I want to be trim, but I can no longer sit in front of a mirror and chastise myself for extra pounds. The value of a person is his/her soul, not the amount of body fat.

Catastrophizing your current state and ignoring your positive reality overwhelms your objectivity. Once you go down the rabbit hole of harshly judging your reality, getting back to the facts will be tough. This kind of swirling, sinking thinking has no purpose except to widen your great internal divide. Keeping your "shoulds" and perceived reality as aligned as possible will make it easier to become a Resiliency Ninja.

Tough times always magnify the gap, so keep it as small as possible. Accepting today and letting go of missed chances will stop your internal tug of war, which makes for one less battle to face when life is hard.

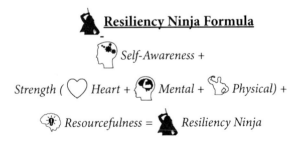

Resiliency Ninja Formula

Self-Awareness +

Strength (Heart + Mental + Physical) +

Resourcefulness = Resiliency Ninja

Are regrets keeping you from being satisfied? If so, what are the "shoulds" that you're expecting from yourself that haven't happened yet?

 Are you falling prey to society and advertisers' idealized perception of how you should live?

 The great internal divide is the distance between "should" and reality. It is the root of unhappiness, frustration, lack of confidence and self-sabotage. The wider the gap, the worse its impact.

 Regret is the "should" of the past. Wallowing in missed opportunities clogs your brain's power to shape your future the way you desire.

 Don't let regrets of the past or desire for the future negate your satisfaction in the present.

 List all your "shoulda, woulda, couldas". Now replace the defeatist word "shoulda" with "want to". If the two can't be interchanged, then rewrite the story for something that you do want and can work towards to make happen.

 Alongside your "shoulda" list write about your current reality. Compare the two. How can you lessen the gap to close the great internal divide?

 Take note of who is influencing your expectations of what reality should be. Is it family, peers, society or advertisers, or do your regrets stem legitimately from your true desires?

18

Can You Hear Me Now?

BEFORE MY SURGERY, I loved the hectic pace of attending more than 200 business events a year, plus writing four newspaper columns a week, plus running an eating-disorder center, plus volunteering, plus having a social life, plus, plus. Now all that busy makes me cringe.

Looking back, I see that pace was unsustainable. There was no way to keep saying yes to everyone else's demands without eventually losing myself in the process. I was so lost in being what everyone else expected me to be that I lost touch with what I truly wanted – and what I was willing to do to get there.

If you live a similar do-it-all lifestyle, I encourage you to ask yourself "Why?" before some traumatic event forces you to ask that question.

Is your pace aligned with who you really are at your core, or are you giving into unrealistic expectations from others or yourself? Whose life are you really living? What are you trying to prove by putting so much on your plate?

It's obvious to me now that when I was rushing around so fast, I was afraid that, if I slowed, I might realize that deep down I was unsatisfied. Being in a constant state of hurry and expecting myself to do something of significance every waking minute meant I missed the guide posts along my path.

Life provides touchpoints of clarity in escalating volume. Ignoring these signs that you've taken the wrong path essentially dares the universe to play "Can you hear me now?" That's when something, somewhere, knocks you down with a strong, unmistakable blow that makes you finally say, "Oh, I see now. It would be better if I went *that* way."

The problem is that when we're moving so quickly, we can't see the clues that guide us toward our life's purpose and fulfillment. That clarity comes when we embrace stillness. Call it prayer or meditation or just stepping away from technology. Making quiet time in your mind can go a long way to setting you on the right path.

I know, easier said than done.

The clues the universe keeps sending you aren't just for big life decisions. Sometimes they come in the form of little nudges that send us in the right direction. I can't tell you the number of times forgetting something at home or missing a green light was a blessing. On some occasions, I've been minutes, even seconds, away from disaster. Recently a friend and I were driving home from an event when she realized she had left her phone behind. By turning back, we missed a huge traffic accident. That forgotten phone was a blessing, even though in the moment it could have caused frustration. When inconveniences like these happen, I just go with the flow and say, "Well, I guess this is the direction I'm meant to take."

It's comforting to me to believe that problems – large or small – are a part of a greater plan. I have a strong faith and believe a higher power is looking out for each of us. It's up to us to choose to listen. Whatever you call "it"—God, the universe, your intuition, or any source that makes you feel comfortable – embrace it. It doesn't have to be about religion, but about finding a way to put the unknown and unexplained in a place that you can trust.

Dr. T. thinks my belief that "the universe unfolds as it's meant to" is gibberish. He says the universe is busy doing other things – like being the universe. It is not actually leaving guide posts. He thinks individuals create their own path. What we notice as "signs," he says, are just the signals we choose to see.

Regardless of your belief, consistently ignoring minor aches, pains and frustrations means you may be overlooking the very arrows that can show you the way.

Long before the surgery, I think my intuition tried a gentler way to nudge me in the right direction. I'd had a few incidents like fender benders and small injuries that were telling me to slow down and make better decisions. These were flags waving me in for a course change, but I was too busy to notice.

I spent the weekend before my life-altering surgery with a man who was not a healthy choice. After I suffered multiple heartbreaks falling for similar types of wrong guys, the universe stepped in and said, "Fine, you're not listening. We'll take care of that."

The surgery was the next day. A few minutes for a minor procedure turned into hours in the operating room. After that the guy was long gone and I was on a path toward recognizing that choosing healthy relationships and setting boundaries with others were skills I'd been missing for a long time.

It took a botched surgery for me to slow down and make better choices about who I wanted to attract into my life and how to streamline my work to be more profitable and require less time. I didn't realize the blessings right away, but they were there.

Another benefit of my surgery: it was one of the catalysts that got me out of writing my *People You Know* column, which is, on the whole, a good thing. Sure, being a columnist offered a lot of perks, and it was important to the influential people whom I featured. But if I'm honest, it was a pretty superficial existence because all I had to do was show up at events, observe people interacting and capture a story in print. The superficiality of the whole effort became apparent soon after I resigned from the column; a significant portion of my network disappeared since I was no longer of use to them.

Once you're out of the spotlight, it's easy to be forgotten. For me, that brought a new set of identity issues to the surface. Even with many so-called friends disappearing, I look back and think, wow, there were blessings that came from the botched surgery. I resigned from the column after the fiascos with my medical situations inspired me to run politically to try to fix the healthcare system. Some may suggest that my jump into politics didn't exactly move me out of the realm of the superficial, but many of my most cherished professional friendships have come through my involvement in politics. When you're in the trenches fighting for a cause you believe in, you bond easily with others. I'm so grateful I met those incredible people with whom I still feel connected, even the ones I don't see often.

Imagine if I had just kept going with my busy-busy writing. My talents as a business consultant may never have emerged, and I would have missed a bunch of adventures that wouldn't have been possible if I had to stay in the city to attend events. And I wouldn't have been forced to re-evaluate how I was running myself ragged.

There were other course corrections along the way. Some client projects went sideways, but now, looking back, I realize that I wouldn't have been happy doing the tedious work those projects required. Losing work may have hurt at the time, but it was worth it in the end. Ultimately, my pain was a gift. The universe knew that I should be on a different path. Although

I still have many bad memories of that period, I'm so glad I had a chance to stop, reassess, and change paths.

Not every accident is a sign. Even so, whenever I stub my toe I take a few seconds to contemplate what I'm doing at that moment, and whether I believe it's a healthy thing to do. Sometimes a stubbed toe is just a stubbed toe; but other times it may be a warning sign that says, "Slow down, and look both ways."

There are days when it feels like the universe is conspiring against me, and even so I find the silver lining in what is happening. For example, the first day I planned to shoot the cover photo for this book, everything went wrong.

My eyebrows had been waxed the day before and were now completely uneven, or more so than usual. I looked like I had two different eyes. That threw off my makeup, which in addition to having to contend with the warped eyebrows that day, just didn't match my natural vibe – even though I had one of the best makeup artists in town. Normally I love having my makeup done, but on that day, it just didn't make me feel my best.

As I left the makeup chair to get Winston from the groomers and then head to the photo studio, the wind started blowing and the rain came down. Of course, I had no umbrella. Now my hair was flat and stringy. I can deal with this, I thought, after all, I'm a Resiliency Ninja.

Winston was scheduled at our favorite groomers for a wash and blow-dry. When I walked in, I couldn't believe what I saw. They had cut his facial hair so short he looked like a sheep, with a little bitty face and huge fluffy body. I called the photographer to see if we could Photoshop Winston's hair back into the photo. He thought that was a bad idea. To top it off, my being late meant he was going to have to rush the shoot because he had another client coming right after me.

As I sat in my driveway with my new sheep baby, I called Mom to express my frustration. She wisely asked, "Is this happening for a reason? Maybe you need to cancel for another day."

I then vented to a friend, and she agreed with my mom. The shoot wasn't meant to happen that day.

So, while my initial response was anger and panic, the follow-up response quickly shifted to, "This will work out as it should. Accept today's signs and relax."

What happened next led to the cover you see today, which I love. The original photographer was too busy to plan a reshoot for two weeks, so I looked for another option. Ultimately, the studio that was recommended to me canceled the day before the shoot. *OMG, universe really? Another delay?* But when I called the makeup artist to cancel she said, "Wait, I have an idea."

A friend of hers, who shoots incredible photos for lululemon, was free the next day at the exact time I had scheduled with the other photographer. She has a beautiful open studio and quickly understood my vision for the cover. An hour later we were booked. Everything was different. My brows were back to normal and Winston's hair had grown back just enough that you couldn't tell he had ever looked like a sheep. The photographer's guidance inspired new wardrobe choices and assured that the picture captured me authentically and in my most energized and joyful state. My original shoot from hell never took place because there was a better plan in the works.

Although it may not be easy to have faith that everything will work out as it should when your original plans are going off the rails, cut yourself some slack. Remind yourself that eventually something good will come out of these turbulent circumstances.

There is always a silver lining in the worst experiences – even when my dad passed away. Although his passing was devastating, it allowed Mom and me to develop a much stronger relationship than we ever had before. Dad and I were so close and talked every day for long conversations, so it didn't leave much room for Mom and me. Once Dad got sick it forced us to communicate frequently, and soon she became my best friend.

Can you see times in your life when everything went wrong, but ultimately it proved a blessing? Next time things seem to be falling apart at the seams, take a moment to contemplate if it's the universe's way of sending you in a better direction.

Have faith that your life is unfolding as it should, and that there are better opportunities just around the corner. During the tough times, these may be the most comforting thoughts you've got. Hang onto them.

Resiliency Ninja Formula

Self-Awareness +

Strength (Heart + Mental + Physical) +

Resourcefulness = Resiliency Ninja

 Do you notice life's guide posts or are you too busy? Looking back, what are some annoyances that turned out to be blessings?

 When situations seem out of place, what sign can be gleaned from the experience? Is your stubbed toe the universe's way of telling you to pay more attention?

 Have faith that life is unfolding as it should.

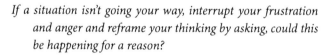 *If a situation isn't going your way, interrupt your frustration and anger and reframe your thinking by asking, could this be happening for a reason?*

 Find stillness to see your guideposts more clearly. Choose the best way that works for you. It could be prayer, meditation, turning off technology, or just looking up when you're walking through your day.

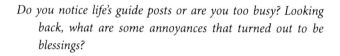 *Write a list of all the times when you were frustrated with how things were going, but something positive came out of the situation. Use this list as a great reminder when the universe nudges you again.*

19

The Roller Coaster of Emotions

I WAS SPEAKING AT A conference located next to a theme park. The day after my session a speaker colleague and I decided to have some fun and try a roller coaster ride. Why not?

I'll tell you why not. Because they're scary as hell.

The absolute lack of control and fearful anticipation of what was coming around the next turn makes my chest pound again just writing about it. The craziest memory is when I felt like I couldn't breathe when we dropped suddenly. I felt like my chest was going to explode.

The kid behind me was really freaking out and desperately wanted off the ride (I swear I wasn't the only one screaming). As we slowed down, one of the attendants on the sidelines comforted the girl by saying, "No worries sweetie, all the scary stuff is over." Moments later we sped up and went for another big heart-stopping plunge.

Bitch.

Isn't that how our emotions can feel? Up and down and all around, testing us at every turn. And just when we think we're through the worst of it, bam! Another drop.

Understanding the cyclical nature of emotions is essential on your Resiliency Ninja journey. Intellectually you can have confidence that even though you are feeling a horrible emotion now, at some point, eventually, it will pass. This allows you to recognize the feeling for what it is – a passing sensation – instead of allowing it to influence your accomplishments for the day. If you allow your feelings to dictate what you do there's a good chance that many days you'll stay in bed, skip work and eat junk food.

Just as we can't hang onto positive emotions all day, the bad ones also subside.

One book that was pivotal on my journey is called *The Happiness Trap: Stop Struggling and Start Living,* by Russ Harris. It points out and I'm paraphrasing here, that we've been sold an idea that the neutral point for our emotional state is happy. Thus, in moments when we aren't elated we judge ourselves as if we are doing something wrong. The truth is, our baseline is neutral, and emotions fluctuate up and down from there. How can we appreciate happiness if we've not felt sadness? I would argue that the deeper the despair felt, the more capacity there is to rebound an equal distance on the other side of the spectrum to appreciate pure joy.

That's likely why I often get compliments from people saying that I seem joyful, content and at peace. Absolutely that's true on many days, but only because I have wallowed in frustration, devastation and boredom enough that I appreciate and honor positive emotions with vigor.

To master your emotions, you first must become clearly aware of them. Then you need to discover the patterns that surround them. You will be able to understand better how and when to change the tunes playing in your head. This knowledge will give you a head start to stabilize your feelings, so your lows aren't so devastatingly low and the highs not so manically high. Even if you still have the swings, you'll be self-aware enough to better navigate rough waters. A sturdy ship is always safer.

I feel every emotion with intensity, so figuring out how to manage the daily emotional roller coaster takes a lot of effort. Just when I think I've got my feelings under control, hormones throw me for another loop. As Dr. T. reminds me, physiology beats psychology.

Just as you can get into conversational ruts with your friends, you can also get into emotional ruts with yourself. You can start looping around and around, getting stuck on a mood that erodes your heart's well-being.

Unless you purposefully identify these traps and interrupt these loops you may never let go. This is how people get stuck. They bask in the sensations over and over until they're anchored in anguish.

Many times, the worst instigator of the roller coaster ride is your own self-sabotaging patterns. You may start to have fun, but then start feeling guilty, perhaps because a friend died, and you want to honor that person by showing your sadness, so you immediately stop having fun. Or you get a big promotion at work or land a huge client, and you don't do a fantastic job because deep down you don't believe you deserve these opportunities. You procrastinate about getting your big project done, filling your days with meaningless busy work because you feel overwhelmed and don't know where to start.

One minute you're soaring, excited about life and work. The next moment you get some unexpected criticism, and it sends you into a tail spin. Been there, done that. But then I began to recognize my pattern of folding whenever I got unfavorable feedback. Understanding this dangerous response allowed me to catch myself before falling into the same trap again, and to get back on track faster.

What are the emotional patterns that keep you flying through the big loops on the roller coaster, or maybe even keep you from ever getting on the ride? I had several loops in my head for a long time, made more extreme by a lack of self-confidence.

One unhealthy pattern that reared its ugly head once in a while took place whenever I sold big contracts. The good news would practically paralyze me. Sounds counterintuitive, doesn't it? I wouldn't send an invoice right away. Then I took my foot off the gas on other sales initiatives, to really ensure I sabotaged my momentum. I felt undeserving. Eventually something would happen, such as a client deadline or a dwindling bank account, to kick-start my efforts. After the next big sale, I'd freeze all over again.

Once I had secured an invitation to write for a major online advice portal. It was HUGE. I was so excited. The editor approved my three ideas for stories. The first column wasn't typical of my usual scope – I was trying too hard because I was intimidated by the opportunity. When the editor emailed me to say she was declining the column because it didn't quite fit their format, and suggested I publish it elsewhere, I was devastated. Instead of tweaking it and submitting the copy to another publication where it would have been a better fit – or at the very least completing and submitting the other two approved columns – I stopped writing anything for publications for more than six months.

Talk about riding the roller coaster of emotions all the way into a nose dive. Not understanding how to manage negative self-talk, handle obstacles, and discipline myself to keep my biz on track, meant that there were big wins followed by big plunges. Thankfully, becoming aware of destructive emotional routines and how they influenced my work outcomes, was the start of me stepping off the nauseating roller coaster ride.

Resiliency Ninja Formula

Self-Awareness +

Strength (Heart + Mental + Physical) +

Resourcefulness = Resiliency Ninja

 What are your patterns around your emotions? Do you react quickly? Do you deflect the most difficult feelings? Do you expect to be happy every minute and think something is wrong when you're not? Do you feel guilt or shame around any of your emotions?

 Feelings are sensations that are cyclical. Just as good feelings pass, so too shall the tough stuff.

 The deeper the depths of despair you've felt, the more capacity you have to rebound to feel an equal amount of pure joy.

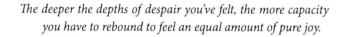 *The base state of your emotions is neutral, not happiness. You can't expect to be happy 24/7.*

 Physiology beats psychology. Don't underestimate the influence hormones or medications can have on your attitude.

Identify looping patterns of emotions that don't serve your best interests. Write them down so you can acknowledge their existence next time you start the loop.

20

The Melting Pot of Emotions

IMAGINE ALL YOUR EMOTIONS TOSSED together in a huge witch's caldron. Happiness, joy, hate, fear, anger, are all boiling in the same pot, like that green goo that witches were always cooking in cartoons when we were kids. The witch would scoop up a grotesque spoonful, have a taste and throw the rest of it back into the pot. She would continue to dip the spoon for more samples as different ingredients would rotate boiling to the top.

That's the trouble with our emotions.

They bubble briefly to the top and then sink back to the bottom of the brew. How long each emotion stays on top depends on how long we scoop them up and focus on them.

Since our emotions tend to blur together, it's difficult to sift through and determine which feelings are tied to each problem and compartmentalize them accordingly. Some negative emotions, such as grief, discouragement, shame and disappointment can be overwhelming and all-encompassing, overshadowing all other issues and feelings. If you're not careful, they will become the lens through which you feel everything.

Managing multiple emotions can be compared to multi-tasking. Your brain really isn't good at doing multiple activities at one time. Successful multi-taskers are just capable of switching between tasks very quickly. I believe emotions act the same way. Your heart can't focus on more than one feeling at a time, so you just switch really quickly between them.

Mastering emotions begins by choosing which feelings to let boil to the top and then sink back down, and which emotions we most want to grab with our spoon to savor.

Do we often feel sad? Absolutely. We just don't want to grab the sad morsel and focus only on it as if it's the only ingredient in the pot. It's best to do everything in our power to locate other, more constructive sensations and focus our efforts there.

Negative emotions are a healthy aspect of life, but they need to be associated with the appropriate cause. Melding all emotions together into a sticky goo and not recognizing each as a separate entity can create a fluid, volatile emotional state that is hard to manage and control. Instead, decipher which emotions are tied to which experiences, and put them into their rightful place.

A breakup is a great example of the sort of incidents that enable our negative emotions to take over in inappropriate ways. Perhaps you've been dumped or had a big fight with your significant other. Suddenly you are in a nasty mood, and that dark cloud taints your every interaction with co-workers. The office is on edge all day because you've got an atypical sharp edge to your personality. The strongest emotion at any moment is the one that the people around you will sense.

A detrimental emotional state will give more power to the Internal Messenger of B.S. Any negative emotion, not dealt with in a healthy way will impact the story you tell about yourself, your talents and your accomplishments. Like most lessons, this one I learned the hard way too.

One of my public-speaking colleagues, whom I met with frequently in our mastermind group, had just hired another person to help her with her business planning. I was surprised she didn't ask me, because I would have gladly helped her. I am pretty good at seeing the holes in people's marketing and sales processes, which is exactly what she needed.

When I asked her about her decision, she told me: "Since you are always complaining about your business in our mastermind sessions, I didn't think you were successful enough to actually help me."

Oh, that stung.

Here I had been complaining about my overall business, but in truth most aspects were going quite well. As an entrepreneur, I have high expectations, and I tended to never be satisfied. By the same token, I had difficulty acknowledging my wins. I may have succeeded in many areas, but I couldn't take my eyes off the failure over there.

My grumbling was evidence that I was continually grabbing massive amounts of disappointment from the cauldron of goo and rubbing that negative goo over the entire business, rather than just spreading it on a few specific areas of frustration.

A better way to handle those masterminds would have been to be clearer about my real struggles. That goo of disappointment that I splashed all around could have more accurately been applied to my real problems: the restraints that my physical limitations put on the amount of business I could accept, and my dwindling interest in repeating the same content over and over.

I was constantly comparing myself to others in the group who were doing training sessions for clients three to five days a week. As a result, I assumed that was the standard it took to be considered successful. Anything less than high volume meant failure.

But I wasn't capable of that pace, so measuring my success against those trainers was pointless. Between consulting gigs, training sessions and keynotes, I was already at full capacity. Add in media, sales activities and prep time for my clients, and I couldn't have handled more even if new opportunities came flying through the door.

Instead of complaining about my business in general, it would have been better if I confided in my colleagues that my pain meant that I was now working at maximum output, which was less than I accomplished pre-surgery. I could have admitted that I thought I was a failure because I wasn't living up to my pre-surgery activity level, and that I needed to learn to leverage my time better. Plus, I was bored out of my mind. Had I shared those concerns, I might have gotten much more useful feedback from my colleagues. All these separate issues were solvable but dealing with the whole confusing pot of goo was not. Dissing my whole business because of capacity and motivation issues wasn't useful.

Until I realized that my business did not deserve the unfair representation I was giving it, and that my negativity was really a disguise for my discontent with my physical limitations, I could not communicate authentically with the other members of my group.

When you feel that you are going into a tizzy about something, stop for a second and ask yourself, "What is this really about? What am I really feeling?" Don't take as gospel the first answer that pops into your head. Keep asking, "Is this emotion really true, and is *this* actually its cause?" Go deeper until you've truly discovered which feelings go with what experiences.

Resiliency Ninja Formula

Self-Awareness +

Strength (Heart + Mental + Physical) +

Resourcefulness = Resiliency Ninja

Do you allow negative emotions to overshadow everything in your life, rather than just apply them to the appropriate circumstances where they belong?

How aware of your emotions are you? Can you correctly identify what emotion you're feeling? Or do they just feel to you like a boiling pot of goo?

When you get into an emotional tizzy, jot down all the emotions you feel. Then decipher which emotions match which issue to apply the emotion to its rightful owner.

The most powerful emotions, such as shame, grief and discouragement, can seep into all aspects of your life if you don't recognize each and associate it with the proper cause.

Multitasking is not possible; the brain just switches quickly between thoughts. Emotions function the same way. You choose which emotion you'll focus on at any given moment. Choose wisely.

21

A Balanced Emotional Diet

ANOTHER WAY TO LOOK AT emotions is to imagine them all as foods in the various food groups such as proteins, grains, vegetables and fruits. If you constantly eat only bread and pasta, because you hate protein and vegetables, your health will dwindle.

At some point, mom was right: you need to eat your vegetables.

The analogy here is simple: if you ignore the emotions you don't like for too long, the universe will force you to deal with them – possibly with an explosive blast of "Can you hear me now?"

I couldn't begin to heal from my adversities until I finally allowed myself to feel the deepest, darkest emotions connected to my most important issues. Before that I was just trying to channel happy feelings, which I did by pushing down all the harshest ones I didn't want to feel. It wasn't healthy. It's like trying to sit on the entire Whack-a-Mole game to hold all the critters down at once, instead of hitting each mole as it pops up. The strongest of the worst emotions – anger, self-loathing, shame, grief– kept trying to pop up despite my best efforts to whack them down. They finally broke through and consumed me.

An early-stage solution was compartmentalizing. Ignore the pain, ignore the grief, and find joy in what's happening in the moment. Take my eyes off my own issues and focus solely on the needs of the person in front of me. That approach helped me power through professionally when I needed to perform. It's still a key strategy when I need to be resilient in the short term. You can feel a sense of emotional control from compartmentalizing, but it's just a short-term fix. It only works if you later focus on the compartments you've shut down and deal with the deepest issues. There really is no escaping feelings of grief, frustration, loneliness or any other emotion you want to pretend doesn't exist.

I found it very hard to feel the deep-deep sadness over losing loved ones, specifically my dad.

Every time I went for a body treatment at a spa or a wellness center, without fail they would mention my heart chakra was blocked. It was as if physically I had created a brick wall of protective energy around my chest. I had subconsciously decided no one was getting in to cause me any more hurt.

If I started to erupt inside, I would force the emotion back down until it was just a tiny inkling of a feeling. I switched the subject in my heart, much like one might abruptly change the topic of conversation. I did that with any emotion I didn't like.

When I finally sat still, without the television to numb my emotions or my mobile phone to distract me, the waterworks started gushing. Surprisingly, the angst I was so afraid to feel proved so comforting when I finally acknowledged it, that I didn't want to turn off the tears. I sobbed uncontrollably. The authenticity freed me. It was like a giant weight was lifted from my heart. With that negative energy foothold gone, I felt less guarded when I was with people. This allowed me to create deeper relationships. Suddenly I was less afraid to be authentic with others and felt less concerned with people seeing the truths behind my curtain.

It's okay to feel anger and hurt. Pain dissipates once we acknowledge it and let it linger long enough to lose its power over us. Emotions are just passing sensations, and they fade much faster when we allow and accept them. You may remember in Chapter 12: *You Can't Fake Forgiveness*, I talked about how to dissolve emotions.

Freeing my personal fears and negative emotions ultimately freed my business and client relationships too.

For a long time, I didn't want to get too close to clients. I preferred to do just one-time keynotes and training sessions for fear that, if they spent too much time with me, they would see my flaws and all the challenges I was dealing with off-stage.

After letting go of pretense and internal judgments, I changed my business to allow longer-term consulting gigs with small-to-medium sized businesses, so I could really get involved in helping them succeed. Before I gained that confidence in getting closer, I mainly worked with huge financial institutions where it was easy to get lost. You'd see trainees once, impart your wisdom, and never see them again. That was safe.

No one ever got close enough to see that I was consumed with hurt, shame and devastation. I was letting my personal adversities and limited emotional wellness impact how I showed up with my clients and in professional scenarios. The irony was that the more I tried to hide my personal problems, the more power I gave to my adversities. They would have had less power if I faced my fears and dealt with the bad stuff when it started.

Thanks to this emotional epiphany, I now compartmentalize less, because I don't have the same fear of feeling negative emotions. Now that I've felt the worst and come out the other side more confident and less guarded, I don't fear vulnerability as I used to. If people see the worst sides of me, that's okay, because the view of me they are getting is the most authentic. If it doesn't resonate with them, then so be it. Now, I don't have to spend the entire relationship worrying about trying to be perfect.

Resiliency Ninja Formula

Self-Awareness +

Strength (♡ Heart + Mental + Physical) +

Resourcefulness = Resiliency Ninja

Which emotions are you most afraid to feel?

What is your ritual for pushing down negative emotions to avoid feeling them?

Instead of deflecting from a difficult-to-feel emotion, allow yourself to feel the full depth of its pain and hurt. Sit with it until it becomes less intense and dissipates.

Sit still. Turn off the TV, the phone, the computer. Don't move until you've felt the worst emotions, processed them and the sensations have dissipated.

What are your techniques to numb out the worst emotions? Write a list of what works for you to deflect emotions, because when it's ON time at work, you can use those tactics to keep you focused on the task at hand.

22

The Plight of the Unsuspecting Innocents

IF YOU RESIST DIFFICULT EMOTIONS for too long, they will eventually explode with a vengeance. When that happens, the force is usually directed at the wrong problem or person. Emotional intelligence trainers might call this an "amygdala high jacking," when your lizard brain forgoes all rational decision making and lashes out in ways that don't align with your personality.

Deflecting and avoidance are natural responses to negative feelings. But until you recognize the hurt, frustration, embarrassment or fear, these forces will all keep bubbling to the top until they find an outlet.

When my dad died, I was a wreck. The grief was overwhelming, so I pretended it didn't exist and went along my merry way. All of a sudden, the printer would jam or someone would take my parking spot or a drive-thru clerk would give me the wrong order, and I would overreact. Since I wasn't dealing with the real problem, small glitches were magnified into huge issues by the emotional impact of the adversity I was trying to bury.

"Don't sweat the small stuff," they say. I think frustration with the small stuff is a sign that you're not dealing with the big stuff. If you're at peace as a person, a printer jam will not wreak havoc.

There have been a few health scares with Mom. After going through brain tumors, lung and other cancers with Dad, I'll admit the idea of losing her is scary especially given how close we've become and how integrated into my life she is. Whenever my mom was in the hospital for her heart problems, I tended to get uncharacteristically short-fused, snappy and aggressive, instead of being supportive and appreciative. Something small would happen, with Mom or someone else, and my typical patience was gone out the window.

It's not fair to others. Intellectually I can see that now, but before it was brought to my attention I was clueless to this pattern. We don't know what we don't know and can't beat ourselves up for the past. Once we see an issue, then we can fix it and prevent it from happening next time.

When you're facing challenging predicaments, you need to get good at quickly assessing situations and finding ways to reset your emotional balance before an unsuspecting innocent gets the wrath of misplaced anger, hurt, frustration, disappointment or any other emotion that may keep you from being your kindest self.

Maybe a friend has abandoned you, but not everyone else has. Yes, you lost your best friend or a family member, but the people in front of you deserve to be cherished. Yes, you broke a bone, but the person who accidentally bumps your cast doesn't need to feel the equivalent pain. Trying to make yourself feel better by causing emotional anguish in people around you will not relieve the intensity of your own pain. Instead, when you feel yourself getting out of control, take a second to check in. Ask yourself, "What's really going on right now?" Intellectually you can reframe that moment to interrupt your bad behavior.

Can you imagine being on the receiving end of the stressed-out drive-through customer who is acting like a forgotten napkin is the end of the world? This employee now has had to suffer the consequences of someone else's shitty day and lack of emotional intelligence.

Years ago, when someone was rude to me or did something out of character, I would assume they didn't like me or I'd done something wrong. Now, I flip the conversation in my head and recognize that since their response is out of character, there is likely something happening in their life that has put them in a mood, and I was just the punching bag they needed. Instead of getting angry about it, I'll send them a quick prayer and hope they feel better soon.

Their actions may not be right, but with the right insight you can avoid having their grouchiness impact your emotional well-being. Realize they're just pushing their unmanaged feelings onto you.

Everyone is trying to navigate his or her own path through life. Even on good days, that path can be hard. Every time we take our negative emotions out on innocent people, the more we pile our obstacles on someone else's life. We may not intend it, but that's really a mean, selfish thing to do. And I believe most people don't want to be selfish or mean.

I know I've been responsible for sending frustrations in the wrong direction at various points in my life. It's not right. In the moment I saw it happening, like a movie, or more accurately like a train wreck that I was helpless to stop. Now, I know, that acting kindly to someone even when feeling devastated about something else, is absolutely within my control.

If I commit this offence now, and it happens rarely now that I'm constantly trying to name my emotion and put it into its proper place, I always try to go back and make it right with an apology and an explanation. That helps people understand and forgive, but it's still better to stop the lash-out before it happens.

To all the innocents out there who have been on the receiving end of such frustration or pain, I'm sorry. Anyone who can look at their actions objectively in these scenarios can say, "It's not you, it's me," and you can believe them. Don't internalize other people's bad behavior.

Resiliency Ninja Formula

Self-Awareness +

Strength (Heart + Mental + Physical) +

Resourcefulness = Resiliency Ninja

 Do you take out your worst feelings on innocents?

 What's the trigger for you to act inappropriately toward innocent bystanders?

 In the moment, when you're angry, go deeper into your heart and identify what you're feeling.

 Interrupt bad behavior by noticing it and taking a moment to reset and reframe the situation.

 Write a list of times you've reacted rudely to innocents because you were upset about something in your life. Rewrite the scenario to determine a different way to react in that circumstance next time.

 If possible, apologize and make amends with any unsuspecting innocents you've hurt.

23

How Badly Do You Want It?

A COUPLE OF TIMES WHEN I've been in the dip of an emotional roller-coaster ride, my mom has asked me if I should give up my business and go get a regular job.

She asks this for a reason. She knows that questioning my commitment reminds me how much I love helping people through my business, and that I want to stay the course. This challenging question immediately shifts me from freeze or flight to fight, from poor-me thinking to solution-finding mode.

My answer has never wavered. My response is, "Absolutely not."

A Resiliency Ninja doesn't quit.

To stand in your best superhero pose in front of a blowing fan of crap takes guts and perseverance. You can overcome any obstacle if you don't give up, but you'll only put in the effort needed if you are really committed to the goals you think you want. When life sucks, staying power requires deep desire.

I think we have all had moments – hopefully fleeting – where we say, "You know what? Maybe it's easier to bail." As a business owner, you wish someone else could carry the headaches for a while, and you might be tempted to walk away. If you're willing to jump ship when there is still a chance to succeed, then you don't want it badly enough to find the resources that will solve your problems.

As an employee, you may wish to throw in the towel and get another job. Sometimes that's the answer – there are always other jobs to be found, but people are the same wherever you go. If you don't work to become your best, most resilient self, then you will just lug your problems with you to your new job.

There are employees I talk to who dream of starting their own business, but hold back for fear of uncertainty. It's only natural that a regular paycheck and benefits may trump the unknown and the possible difficulties it can bring.

What's not comforting over the long haul is living most of your life being unhappy at work. We spend way too much time grinding away at our jobs to dislike doing it. There is so much potential in today's global economy to be your own boss, or to find a new employer who respects employees. So please don't limit yourself to thinking that where you are is the only place you can be.

If changing jobs is not an option, then adjust your attitude towards what you are doing. If you're miserable in your work, if it doesn't speak to your soul or feed your desires, then that adds a layer of struggle atop all the things that already suck in your life.

Start taking responsible steps to really be happy in your workplace. Make a list of requirements for your current role. Next, decide which tasks you enjoy and which cause you the most stress. Then identify ways to deal with the stressful stuff by delegating, changing or streamlining the tasks, so you can tilt your job to be more enjoyable. Sometimes the only option you have is to shift your approach to the work and find a rhythm that makes the days go faster.

If you don't believe that your work can ever align with your passions, then at least make it a neutral influence, instead of hating it and having that negativity cloud your life and zap your energy. Begin to approach any less-than-desirable tasks at work as things you just must do, like brushing your teeth. The important thing is that when you are faced with these jobs you don't like, get right to them and complete them well. Adding procrastination to the mix would only prolong the pain. Then, satisfaction from accomplishing the project may boost your morale. It may also be helpful to get right to the bottom line, reminding yourself that they are part of the responsibilities you need to fulfill so you'll get your next pay cheque. Perhaps considering the money will get the jobs done faster, easier and with less drama. The unpleasant aspects of a job description are collateral damage that simply comes with the package. Plus, remember that you can find joy outside of your job, by volunteering, or engrossing yourself in side projects or hobbies.

Some success coaches will tell you it all comes down to having a compelling "why" that drives you. Dive deep into your "why." Coaches will ask variations of these questions, "*Why do you do what you do? What's your greater purpose in life?"* umpteen different ways. While I admire people who have succinct and inspirational answers, finding my overarching "why" feels strenuous. In fact, I'm not sure I'm even there yet. It's such a frustrating exercise that I stopped booking calls with one of my business coaches because we just kept going around in circles as he asked me twenty different ways to articulate some profound statement of "why." Every time I tried to articulate my "why" it felt like a forced attempt at being inspirational. It just wasn't passing my gut check.

My "why" is basically because this is what I'm meant to do, it's that simple.

I love speaking on stages, and I easily get lost in the creative process of writing. Communicating and being creative make me tick. I feel compelled to help people succeed by getting out of their own way, probably because I spent so much time putting up my own road blocks. I really want to catch people before they fall into the victim trap, because it's a miserable place to exist. But is that really my "why," or is it just what I'm trying to achieve? This is where this "why" journey gets my goat; I never know when I have the right answer.

On the business side, I love helping people solve one of the biggest obstacles in business – how to connect with more buyers and influencers. I find it easy to see the holes in a client's plan and it provides great revenue.

Are those compelling enough reasons why I do what I do? I'm not sure they are, but I'm okay with that.

I'm sharing this frustration with you because there seems to be huge pressure in the self-help world to know your "why" and articulate it for all the world to hear. Many of my coaching clients have shared this with me, so if you feel that way, you're not alone. Hopefully my admitting that it's been a point of struggle of me, and others, will relieve some pressure on you if you're struggling with the same concept. Sometimes paying the bills, supporting your family and enjoying your work are ample motivators for the work you do.

I also wonder if the answer to "why" is like faith. Faith isn't always easy to articulate, but you know it's there, and it drives you to stay the course, no matter what gets in your way.

Even without a clear, deep and inspirational answer to "why", you'll still need to be clear on what you want to achieve, and your level of commitment. Ask yourself how badly you want what you want and if you're willing to stay the course even when the proverbial fan powers on high.

Many people are more likely to stay focused on their goals when they make themselves accountable to someone else. When others are counting on you, it's easier to stay motivated and deliver on time. Sometimes the "why" that drives my day-to-day is simply the fact that another person is counting on me. That external expectation seems to be as compelling as any internal big vision that seems light years away.

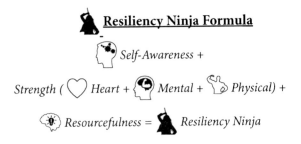

Resiliency Ninja Formula

Self-Awareness +

Strength (Heart + Mental + Physical) +

Resourcefulness = Resiliency Ninja

 Is what you're doing what you want to be doing now and for the rest of your life? If not, what scenarios would make you enjoy your work more?

 How badly do you want what you want? Are you willing to stay the course no matter what road blocks get in your way, or have you got one foot in and one foot out?

 In what direction is your heart pulling you? Go there.

 Have you been able to articulate your "why" motivation? What is it? If not, do you still have a sense of what you want to achieve?

 List all your role responsibilities. Which activities energize you and which drain you? How can you shift the draining tasks to be less taxing or delegate them, or trade job responsibilities?

24

Talk Yourself In, Don't Talk Yourself Out

I DON'T WANT YOU TO think my life was problem-free before my decade of hell. I'm embarrassed to admit I'd had several other physical injuries; a dislocated pelvis from a boating accident and torn ligaments in my shoulder from an earlier skiing accident come to mind. The heartbreaks, the eating disorder and frequent failed attempts at succeeding at jobs and starting small businesses all have a special place in my memory.

There were lots of difficult times. Given all the bumps, sometimes I'm still surprised that I persisted and achieved success. One saving grace early in my career was that I had a naïve belief that I was striving towards something that would make a positive impact on society – even when I was working in mundane jobs, was shy and lacked direction. I may not have been able to articulate it, but I knew eventually something good would happen.

There was a time when I was plagued by insecurities. In my comfort zone when I knew my role – entertainer, mother hen, provider of drinks as a bartender – I would shine. Inside, however, I was self-conscious and often felt like I didn't belong. The reason I loved bartending and waitressing so much was that I felt useful while I was socializing. Since I had a purpose – to bring the beer – people would talk with me. Same thing when I wrote the *People You Know* column. I felt more confident going to events because the people there needed me for positive media coverage.

It's interesting though. Despite having felt that way about myself, if you told me that for you to feel worthwhile in a room you needed a task, I would correct you and try to convince you otherwise. I would tell you, with absolute conviction, that just being you is totally enough. Isn't it funny how we see ourselves through a harsher lens than we see others?

This lack of confidence meant at an early age I had to hone my social skills to restrain myself from retreating and giving up. One day, I'll never forget it, I was having a pity party in the shower when I decided that was enough. I'd failed at some little business venture – I think I was selling makeup – and I had thrown in the towel after deciding I wasn't good enough. With suds in my hair, I decided that the next time an opportunity presented itself I would talk myself *in*, not repeat my pattern of talking myself *out*.

Within a week, I saw an ad for an executive assistant's job for the vice-president of a manufacturing company. Knowing I had to get out of the bar lifestyle, I talked myself into applying. A few days later I was interviewed and hired on the spot. That was the start of a new direction for my life.

Fast-forward a couple of years. I had started building a strong professional network and was working as a fundraiser for an international charity. My boss Margaret and her boss Larry were very supportive and could see that I really wanted to make a positive impact and build personal credibility in the community. They gave me a lot of freedom in my role as a junior fundraiser. Through some of my newly developed connections we had been featured a few times in the popular *People You Know* column which, at the time, was written by a journalist, Carol Kehoe.

Rumors were swirling that Carol was choosing to leave the column and Margaret and I were worried that we wouldn't get coverage for an upcoming event. I called a friend at the newspaper to get the scoop. His immediate response was: "Why? Do you want to take it over?" I laughed, said no and that was the end of that… for a few minutes.

When I told Margaret she chuckled and said, "Aren't you the girl who is going to talk yourself into opportunity? That sounds like a pretty good opportunity to me." I called my friend back to change my answer, "Well, actually, yes, I would like to take over the column." He said, "OK. You have the personality for it, but can you write?" "Of course, I can write," I said. "I just wrote an email." Talk about näivety at its finest. "OK, good luck," he said. "I'll put in a good word for you, but after that, you're on your own."

Moments later I called the Editor-in-Chief and left a voicemail to let him know I'd send him my first column later that night. It took me a week to submit it.

Winning the column wasn't as easy as one phone call, of course. Ultimately it took five months of committed effort, seven mock columns and landing an invitation to a Royal event that the media weren't invited to before I got the job. Those five months were worth every minute of effort to earn the role as the *People You Know* columnist. It gave me an opportunity that I couldn't have dreamed of for myself.

Those 10 minutes changed my life because I went for it. I ignored all the reasons why I shouldn't have even tried. I hadn't written professionally before. Many more qualified people were interested in being the columnist. I had a full-time job plus volunteer commitments, meaning I already had enough on my plate. The list of potential excuses was long, but I ignored them all and said, "Why not? What if?"

What if I didn't get the column in 2003? What if I had applied and the editor chose someone else? I probably would have stayed on my path and looked for another opportunity. At least I would have been confident that I had done my best. If I had not applied I know I would be sitting here with a lot of regret. Perhaps I would never have developed my writing skills and wouldn't be writing my third book. No doubt I wouldn't have done as much media work, for example my weekly radio segment, my stint as a reporter on local television, and other on-air appearances over the years, and there's a good chance Elevate Biz never would have been born. All because, in a matter of minutes, I changed "no" to "yes," and talked myself in.

How about you? How many times have you had an idea, or someone casually made a suggestion for something you would really like to do—and you dismissed it rather than giving it serious consideration and taking action? You could have talked yourself out of your next big break, because you're too scared to learn the answer to "what if?" When the odds are stacked against you and you're afraid you're not good enough, you're likely to retreat unless you make a conscious commitment to talk yourself in.

I believe that an opportunity appears in front of you for a reason; it's up to you to embrace it by evaluating it and, if it speaks to your soul, giving it a chance.

One reason you may ignore opportunity is a fear of failure. Why does the wholly imagined dread of a bad outcome to a potentially positive experience have such a powerful pull? Does it really need to be so strong? Success cannot happen without previous experience at failing.

If you added all my failures, mistakes and embarrassing moments, you'd have reason to call me a Failure Ninja instead of a Resiliency Ninja. Yet each misstep taught me a valuable lesson or sent me in a new direction, making each failure worthwhile.

As we get older and have some failures under our belt, we become conditioned to allow those past experiences to protect us from hurt and disappointment in the future.

Failure is not the essence of who you are. It's merely a snapshot of your circumstances at a moment of time. A failed opportunity went sideways only because you didn't have the right tools, you weren't ready, or hadn't learned the right lesson to get a better outcome. Now you know for next time.

As life started throwing adversity in my direction, maintaining this "talk myself IN" attitude became more difficult. Often, I had to catch myself talking myself out of an opportunity before I could even figure out if I wanted to give it a try.

My physical and emotional pains started to dictate what I would and would not do. At times grief and guilt would overwhelm my sense of adventure and hold me back from activities that might have brought joy. Client expectations that I would continue to teach networking strategies kept me from taking a leap and shifting gears on my service offerings to allow me to grow as a business owner and as a person.

Any guesses as to what holding myself back felt like? Suffocating. Inauthentic. Defeatist. Catching this pattern was important. Once I did, it reignited my spark. I know it will for you too.

If you feel blasé about life, chances are you've become good at ignoring new opportunities and staying in your comfy little box amidst familiar surroundings. Perhaps you've forgotten what it's like to take a risk and see the world with enthusiasm and optimism.

Being willing to say yes doesn't automatically mean you're going to notice and embrace opportunities rather than let them pass by. So many people are busy running on their hamster wheels that they're completely oblivious to the amazing potential around them. Why play in a small pond when you could be leveraging this global economy? The world is your pond. There is nothing you can't achieve if you're willing to talk yourself into doing the right activities.

This doesn't mean you should say yes to everything. The purpose of the "talk yourself in" mantra is to make sure you don't miss the most meaningful opportunities that you truly desire for your life.

If taking the trip of a lifetime, opening your own business, writing a book, doing the media interview or climbing a mountain are important to you, then go for it. If grief has taught me anything it's that life is short and meaningful experiences connect us to the rest of humanity. Why not embrace all that the world has to offer?

Point is, if you are going to say no to something important, make sure it's because saying no serves YOUR best interest and not because you believe you aren't good enough, feel you don't deserve it, or think greatness is reserved for someone else. Most of all, be sure it's not the uninvited peanut gallery of judges who hold you back from taking your leap of faith. Fear of failure is compounded by the loudest voices, external or internal, which try to keep you from finding your best, most authentic and successful self.

During tough times, you may feel that the better idea is to retreat to reduced expectations, but it's not. It's pushing through and blowing away the walls of your comfort zone that will give you new skills and an unshakable spirit that helps you overcome your problems faster. In the long run, staying confined in today's comfort zone will lead to an unfulfilled life.

Take a chance. Ignore the voice that typically talks you out of opportunity, and talk yourself IN.

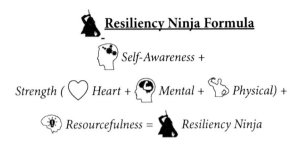

Resiliency Ninja Formula

Self-Awareness +

Strength (♡ Heart + Mental + Physical) +

Resourcefulness = Resiliency Ninja

 Do you talk yourself out of opportunities, using past failures as benchmarks, before you even decide if you want to talk yourself in?

 What are the boundaries of your comfort zone today? What edges are you staying safely inside of, when deep down you know you need to take a leap of faith?

 Is the lingering hurt from past failures weighing heavy on your heart? When opportunities are presented, how does your heart react?

 Write "Talk Yourself IN, Don't Talk Yourself Out." on a Post-It® Note that you see every day.

 Sit with the embarrassment and hurts from past failures, and let your heart know that it's okay.

 Train your body to leap into faith by taking action.

 Identify past failures that are holding you back. Then write all the lessons you've learned from those experiences that will better prepare you for new opportunities in the future.

25

The Uninvited Peanut Gallery of Judges

IF YOU'VE EVER WATCHED OR read any of Brené Brown's work on shame and vulnerability, you may already be aware of how she dealt with the naysayers. After she went viral with her 2012 Ted Talk "The Power of Vulnerability" (27 million views on YouTube!), millions of us took her message to heart. She changed my life by helping me realize and accept that no one is perfect, and it is okay to not be okay.

Unfortunately, this incredibly brave, respected human being felt the wrath of the Internet lynch mob. In an interview called "Bravery & Authenticity" in a Digital World," with Chase Jarvis on Chase Jarvis LIVE, Brené shared how difficult it was to be on the receiving end of internet trolls after she went viral. The way she combats the negative internet trolls is by referencing a special list she carries in her purse. It's a short list of the names of the people whose opinion matter to her. When the naysayers come into view she can refer to the list. If they aren't on it, she will ignore their opinion. It takes discipline and emotional awareness to be able to let go of the nasty opinions of others.

If you're authentic, the right people will find and resonate with you and your message.

Talking yourself IN is a muscle; so is talking yourself OUT and making excuses. What prevents you from saying yes to an opportunity? It's usually not the first three excuses you make. If you want to succeed, there is something deeper than the surface resistance that prevents you from taking the leap of faith. Is it the fear of what others will think? Deep down, it's often a misguided belief that you are not good enough to truly step into your essence. You ARE. Who you are at this particular time is exactly who you need to be, and all the unwelcomed messengers of bullshit can't change that.

Naming your resistance for exactly what it is allows you to blow through your limiting beliefs and make bolder choices.

It's not just strangers or acquaintances who pass uninvited judgments. The worst is when people present you with subtle passive-aggressive opinions. Those can really influence your perception of yourself if you let them.

Many of my doctors used to comment on how I always carried a ton of work with me to my appointments. Their default opinion was that I was a workaholic and needed to relax. This really bothered me. In truth, what they didn't understand was that I couldn't waste precious time in their waiting rooms doing nothing of value. If I had to be vertical, dammit, it'd better be worth my while. Why would I sit there waiting for them and not work towards meeting my deadlines?

Why should I let their opinions make me feel like something was wrong with me because I worked in their waiting rooms instead of sitting around waiting?

We have to be careful about whose opinion we allow to influence our actions and our self-esteem. Those doctors didn't pay my bills. They didn't necessarily know my story, and they couldn't see the vision I had for my future despite the pain. So why did I internalize their opinions as if they have some secret knowledge about me that I couldn't see?

It's human nature to want to feel accepted and validated, I get that. But I also believe there are many people in the world who will accept us for exactly who we are. We need to spend more time finding and associating with those people, and less time accepting criticism from people who make us feel like dirt.

Figuring this out was a turning point. The first thing was to determine whose opinions I truly cared about. As I get older, that list becomes much shorter.

A friend and I were talking a while back, and I was being harsh on myself, as I often used to be. Her question to me was exceptionally powerful. She asked me, "Who is shaping your beliefs about who you are supposed to be?" Good question. So, I am asking you the same one.

Worrying about the periphery just lends itself to a superficial life. *(Sidebar: when I just typed superficial, I actually wrote "suffericial." It's an ironic mistake, because deep down I believe that a superficial existence is a type of suffering. Hmm...)*

Once you know whose opinions matter to you, then turn off everyone else's access to your inner self. Filter any hurtful reviews, stop asking for gossip updates, and avoid conversations with people who are negative or unsupportive. It took me a while to truly grasp that, just because someone says something doesn't make it true.

I comment on local radio stations quite routinely – at least 4 to 5 times a month, sometimes more. With media, especially when it's live, anything can happen.

One of the by-products of caring less about what "they" think is that I've lost a bit of my politically-correct filter, which brings new energy – and new risk – to my media work. It just feels so much more freeing to say what I want to say, rather than muting myself against society's expectations.

But you have to be careful. In one radio interview, I substantially disagreed with the talk-show host on the hot topic of the day. There was no upside for me. If I agreed with the announcer's attack on the person at the center of the news story, I was kicking a politician and friend, when he was down. If I disagreed with the host, I risked being fodder for attacks from callers. In hindsight, this was one media interview I should have declined.

I did my 10-minute commentary on air and then rushed to a doctor's appointment. Unbeknownst to me, the radio host used pieces of my interview throughout the remainder of the show. Callers were not happy with me at all for defending the person they were looking to hang.

It wasn't until the next week that I started to hear rumblings from listeners who wanted to know if I was OK after the radio assault. Blindsided! I was so happy I didn't know about it while it was happening. I had said my two cents worth on air. What the faceless, nameless, peanut gallery calling into a radio show afterward think of me is just a distraction. There's no value in me trying to fix it. It's in the past. Sure, I can learn from it. Beyond that, however, any worries about it or people's opinions of me would just take up unnecessary space in my mind. Now I know I'll decline interviews that are not in my area of expertise, and I will be more guarded with this talk-show host.

The more you buy into trying to appease everyone else's opinions, the less comfortable you'll be in your own space. While losing your politically correct filter can backfire on you as it did on me, it's worth it, and you can stand by who you are by clearly identifying who you will allow to influence your path. Figuring this out in advance is the reason I was not fazed by this hiccup.

Any opinions that don't serve your vision in a constructive way aren't worth your focus.

Take this book, for example. The negative voice inside my head did its best to talk me out of sharing my personal story to you, especially the stories that make me the most vulnerable and have the most potential for embarrassment. More than once the voice has ventured into the area of, "OMG what will 'they' think?"

I had to remind myself that there is no value in letting the cynics and critics influence what I know in my heart to be right. It's up to each of us to protect ourselves from the uninformed opinions of others, and especially to resist joining their chants of disapproval.

Given my sometimes Saran Wrap-thin skin, I wish I could say that I don't care what they think. But if I'm being honest with myself, and with you, I admit I do care, deep down. The question is, do I care enough to let the imagined "they" stop me? No. Please don't let them stop you, either.

What keeps me going is the stronger motivation and a bigger vision than my internal demons can see. A motivational voice inspires me to keep writing because I know that for every person who judges my message, there are countless others for whom it will resonate. Those are my people. The men and women who want to know they aren't alone in having self-judgments, self-doubts and frequent stumbles. They are the ones who want to recognize and accept all aspects of life and respect my decision to pull back the curtain.

The greater good must win over the catty few.

Resiliency Ninja Formula

Self-Awareness +

Strength (Heart + Mental + Physical) +

Resourcefulness = Resiliency Ninja

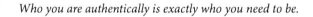

 Whose opinion do you let influence your life?

Whose voices are in your uninvited peanut gallery of judges? Why do you care about their opinion? What would happen if they never approved of your path? Would you still be okay?

Who you are authentically is exactly who you need to be.

 What do you do differently because you're worried about what other people think?

 Make a short list of the people whose opinions you care about. Review it whenever you get uninvited negative feedback. If your naysayers aren't on it, ignore their comments.

26

Cutting the Cords of Self-Sabotage

WHAT'S GUARANTEED TO MAKE LIFE harder than any adversity is the unfortunate, arguably universal, belief that you are not good enough. You are.

At what point in our lives did we learn to downplay our value?

Give someone a compliment and 9 times out of 10 their response diminishes the good wish. "What a lovely hat." "Oh, this old thing?"

Don't deflect compliments. Instead, just say "Thank you," and glow with pride that someone noticed what you did right.

I spent years completely consumed by the thought that I was deeply flawed, and everyone else was not. I felt guilty when I believed I was good at something, because it just didn't feel right. I felt that recognition of my own strengths made me arrogant or vain.

This phenomenon can be traced back to grade school. Whenever you got too big for your britches, a school mate would knock you down. Eventually we learn to do that for ourselves. At least I did.

My immediate family spent most holidays travelling up north to see my Grandma and the rest of our clan. Among my many cherished memories was spending our days at the small ski hill in the area. Since I skied my parents bought me an Ocean Pacific ski jacket for Christmas. I absolutely loved it. Today that means nothing, but when I was in Grade 6 that was hip, especially for a small-town kid who grew up around farm land with no ski hill in sight.

It turns out my "designer" jacket was too hip for some nasty school kid(s), because when I grabbed my coat for recess I noticed a big hole had been cut out of the front left side. I spent the rest of the year and two ski seasons with a patch sewn on the front of my jacket. It was a constant reminder that when I had a little success it would upset others so much that they would take scissors to cut away my enthusiasm. Ultimately, I started cutting myself down emotionally, so I didn't have to go through the hurt of having someone else do it for me. As an adult, I can now look at this situation objectively. As a kid, it was devastating, and just one experience that helped shape my habit of self-sabotage.

While that story was about an inanimate object, the lesson was loud and clear and overflowed into all aspects of my life. It was a horrible way to exist.

Each success triggered an unhealthy internal dialogue. Will this upset anyone? Should I feel bad for this achievement? How can I taper who I am and what I've done so as not to upset others?

The regular knocks of growing up continually reinforced this behavior.

Recently, Mom reminded me of the day I came home with a test that had two separate marks on it – 97 percent and 64 percent. Confused, she pushed me to explain why the teacher's mark wasn't the only one on the paper. What happened was, I added the lower grade to the sheet so that when my friends and I compared test scores I could cover the 97 percent with my thumb and boast a lower grade. I guess getting a 64 percent made me more relatable and was my attempt to make someone else feel better about herself by diminishing myself.

Doesn't that feel like life sometimes? We work hard to do well, and then because we're worried about the perception of others we obscure our achievement.

In Grade 7 our big project was to create a story around what we imagined our life will be like as adults. OMG, I loved that assignment. I cut out images of my gorgeous husband and our five kids from Seventeen magazine. I think for the twins I used the image of the girls from my Sweet Valley High books. The collage included a ranch with horses, a private jet, and other centerpieces of a millionaire, perhaps billionaire, lifestyle. My teacher's response? "You'll need to curb your enthusiasm for life, Allison. No one gets all of that."

I was crushed. Like so many others, I started believing I should think smaller and lost the vision to strive for grandiose dreams.

Many people resist recognizing their own talents and successes, believing that real success is reserved for others; that it's just a figment of the imagination, concocted for a school-kid's patchwork.

Perhaps you play small, talk yourself out of opportunities, and pretty much convince yourself that you're not worthy, even when you're given an award or a promotion.

Society's expectation is that we downplay our achievements and stay in the box we've been provided. No wonder people who believe their own praise are chastised as arrogant. I'm not saying humility isn't a virtue, but damn, sometimes you just have to stand in your power and own it.

There is an abundance of opportunity in the world. The reason you don't take hold of everything the universe has to offer is because of your limiting beliefs. How does someone else deserve more than you think you do?

Limiting beliefs such as "It's all been done before so why bother trying to make a sale, start a business, or make the world a better place?" have the power to hold you back from reaching your true potential.

Sure, there are umpteen books on resiliency, but none of the others have Winston C. on the cover or my decade of hell as a backdrop for the lessons learned. There are so many people in the world: some will click with my message and some will not, and that's okay. It's the same with your work. Even though other people may be doing similar things, there is still a group of people itching to get your version of the topic, product or service.

I consider the thousands of coaches, consultants and speakers out there who charge incredibly high fees, even though many of them were flat broke a few years before. Quite frankly, many of them have no more talent than anyone else; they just happen to be willing to consistently serve their ideal clients and ask big money for doing so.

It's an attitude that allows abundance into your life. Believe you deserve it and embrace it when it arrives.

Resiliency Ninja Formula

Self-Awareness +

Strength (Heart + Mental + Physical) +

Resourcefulness = **Resiliency Ninja**

 Do you have a tendency to self-sabotage? What are some early experiences that taught you to diminish your success?

Close your eyes and imagine, what's the absolute pinnacle for success you feel you are destined for in life?

 Notice when you are sabotaging yourself and interrupt the pattern.

27

Confidence over Self-Sabotage

LATER IN THIS BOOK I'LL come clean about the terrible messages I used to say to myself. This will help you understand how big a leap it was for me to create confidence and to start believing in myself. It was difficult to recognize my talent; I kept knocking myself down to keep myself in check. To start, I had to stop confusing confidence with arrogance. Believing in your self-worth is different than being conceited. Knowing your unique brilliance which you have to offer those around you is not being egotistical; it sets you on a path to self-realization and allows you to step into your personal power. That's a good thing.

Owning your brilliance and accomplishments does not mean you are oblivious to your faults. In fact, true confidence allows you to recognize and accept your genius and your flaws at the same time. It also gives you an objective perspective to quiet the powerful destructive habits that afflict so many of us.

In my work, I recognize that there are certain ways I can serve clients well, and there are other areas where I'm just not talented. Knowing where I shine and where I don't means that I can recommend others who can fill in those blanks, rather than me trying to be all things to all people.

It's hard to become a Resiliency Ninja without recognizing the duality within ourselves. As we approach our goals, it's not unnatural to then do something to avoid achieving the desired outcome. It's a constant conflict that plays simultaneously within ourselves. That is, while parts of us want to win and want to shine, our destructive instincts want to shut us down and hide our light.

To recognize your self-sabotaging routines and change them, make a list of the areas where you resist success and default to self-doubt. Bring these unhelpful beliefs into the light by writing out "I'm not good enough to..." statements. Go as deep and granular as you can with this list. Then you can rewrite the manuscript of your life to counter all this conditioned negative thinking.

For example, *I'm not good enough to*...mingle confidently at a party. Flip that to identify what you are good at instead. I'm good at recognizing when someone is having a rough day, therefore I can try to provide a reason to make that person smile.

Articulating this talent allows you to be in a room and take special notice of people's moods. If they don't look happy, you can waltz over and be extra kind. This will give you a sense of purpose, which feeds your confidence and gives you a reason to forget your insecurities and other issues blowing up behind the scenes.

Early in my career, Mary – a co-worker, friend and mentor – taught me a smart trick. Every time someone gives you a compliment, or you achieve something that makes you feel proud, however small it is, write it down and keep a special "Kudos-to-Me" file. Imagine if you had a collection of all the positive moments in your life that you could look to for positivity and strength when the world throws you curve balls.

In my book *From Business Cards to Business Relationships: Personal Branding and Profitable Networking Made Easy*, I recommend you create a list of 20 of your most positive attributes to remind yourself why people are fortunate to know you. This confidence-building exercise helped me when I was just beginning to make my way in the professional environment, and my self-doubt was toxic.

Daily confidence can be an internal push-pull struggle since society expects you to downplay your talents – countering your authentic desire to bask in your true brilliance. People don't know what to do with someone who has true confidence. Believe it or not, I got to the point where a young guy told me that if I weren't so confident, I'd be more likely to attract a man. Ouch!

People often label those with a strong confidence and its by-product, presence, as intimidating. Unfortunately, this happened to me a lot, and I found it offensive. Just when I would start feeling comfortable in my own skin, it would backfire. I would get labeled as intimidating, which I take as a passive-aggressive insult. I finally realized, I'm not threatening anybody; those others must lack confidence, or else they wouldn't be worried about my opinion of myself.

Perhaps sometimes I come off as too confident, and others interpret that as arrogance, but should I really care? Is it better to continue to hate oneself and conform to society's expectation that we hide our light under a bushel? If someone pays me a compliment, I will validate it with a "Thank you for noticing," and a huge smile. I'm not going to argue with them and tell them their observation is incorrect. Heck, no. All that does is sabotage confidence. I'll own it and savor the positive energy that comes from their kindness, recognizing the fragile emotions behind our humanity. I pay it forward by finding thoughtful praise to share to brighten someone else's day. I call this being a "spark for smiles." and try to make at least one stranger smile each day.

Please know, once you create confidence it's not like you will never experience self-doubt again. Nor does it mean that you won't repeat old patterns for self-sabotage. Obstacles will get in your way and failure will find you. An outside influence can rock you. But don't stay jolted for long. Boost yourself up again, remind yourself of your talents, and get back on track, moving towards your personal vision.

Self-doubt is an epidemic. I wish there was a magic wand that made everyone see their gifts, except there is no magic wand. Each of us has to do the work to learn to believe in and love ourselves. How we show up for people can have a profound impact on how they see themselves. Anytime we can inspire others to notice and embrace their brilliance and the value they have to offer the world is a beautiful moment that shines the light back on your soul. It's a cool way to live.

Resiliency Ninja Formula

Self-Awareness +

Strength (Heart + Mental + Physical) +

Resourcefulness = Resiliency Ninja

Do you believe confidence is the same as arrogance? In your opinion, where is the line between them?

Notice your talents and appreciate them every day.

Look for ways to brighten others' day by giving genuine compliments.

Creating confidence doesn't mean you will never experience self-doubt again.

Practice your thank-you-muscle for compliments. When someone says something nice to you, instead of arguing with them, say thank you and internalize their kindness.

Make a list of at least 20 of your qualities and why someone would be blessed to have you in their life. Review it when you feel self-doubt brewing.

Start a Kudos-To-Me File to capture compliments, awards, small accomplishments and praise to reference for a quick pick-me-up.

28

Personal Attack Ads

THERE'S A COMMANDMENT THAT SAYS, "Love thy neighbor as you love yourself." A friend of mine jokes, "Hell no. If I loved my neighbors as I love myself, my neighbors would move very quickly."

Maybe that commandment should be reversed. If only we could love ourselves as much as we do everyone else, then society as a whole would be much more peaceful.

If I said to you what I've said to myself about myself, we would not be friends. Out loud to someone else, our thoughts – at least mine – could be considered verbal abuse. These personal attacks are the result of the Internal Messenger of B.S. that we talked about earlier. Left to its own devices, the Internal Messenger of B.S. will spew negative stories about yourself, attacking your vulnerabilities while completely ignoring your talents. Whereas we'd reverse it with others whom we admire by only focusing on their strengths and blurring over their negative qualities. The standards to which we hold ourselves are significantly more aggressive than we expect from others. We accept beauty in everyone else and deny it in ourselves. Why are we our own worst enemies?

When I started meeting with Dr. T., he picked up on the cruelty of my self-directed language patterns. I talked about myself very severely. At times, horrifically. I was stuck between denial and anger and it was all wrapped in a bow of self-hatred.

It was as if I was running a presidential-level political attack ad campaign on myself and believing the bad messages. Every hateful comment I said to myself made it more difficult to cope with the external challenges coming at me. Fixing the habit of self-attack was difficult, but I hope that if you can relate you'll take steps to fix these patterns too. Until you do, it's impossible to truly be at peace with yourself and reach your true potential. A Resiliency Ninja does not pick fights with himself or herself.

The self-scathing attack ads are the result of the huge gap between your unrealistic expectations of where you thought you should be at this moment in your life, including unhealthy comparisons to where you think everyone else is and your perceived reality of where you actually are which is often negatively underestimated. If there were no gap you would have no reason to chastise yourself.

One of my vices when my pain spikes, when I am trying to tune out grief or avoid the stress of business, is to watch TV. Most of the time I don't even like the shows I am watching. I can just zone out and let the television do my thinking. For a long time, I literally hated myself while I was lying there. It was a push-pull of internal judgment. The messenger of bullshit would attack me saying, "What kind of a loser sits for hours in front of the TV, escaping life? You should be doing something more productive with your time." Then my kinder internal voice would pipe up with a softer, more compassionate view: "Your body is healing, you have no choice. Right now, you're no good to anyone. Zone out and come back later, refreshed."

It was in those vulnerable moments when I would exaggerate and say horrible things to myself about myself. Sadly, there were also many days when I wasn't feeling vulnerable, and yet I still said stuff like this when I passed a mirror: "*I'm so fat. My extra weight is disgusting; hell, I'm disgusting. I'm so lazy. I'm a sloth sitting around watching TV instead of running my business. I'm weak, giving into pain. I deserve the pain. I'm a failure. Undisciplined. Ridiculous. Uninspired.*"

Do any of these sentiments sound familiar?

The internal dialogue of self-loathing unless we attain perfectionism must stop. It's not fair to believe that if you aren't perfect at one thing you want to achieve, then you must be awful at everything.

Typing those phrases has made my heart race. How could I have spent so many years talking to myself so harshly? By the way, those phrases started long before my decade of hell. In fact, if I hadn't had the surgery, I'm not sure I would have ever had to confront my unhealthy inner dialogue.

I sincerely hope that the words I used to describe myself don't sound familiar to you and that you've never allowed yourself to say horrible things like those to yourself about yourself. Even a hint of harshness in negative self-talk can influence your day-to-day experiences and your confidence.

There are two ways to counteract these negative voices. The first is to get the voices out of your head by capturing how you talk to yourself on paper. The second step is to flood your mind with alternative messages that encourage a healthier relationship with yourself.

Once I was aware of the mean-spirited comments I made about myself, I would write them down or say them out loud, and then decide if I would say or write the same thing to a friend. Usually the answer was never. If I won't say it to a friend, then I won't accept saying it to myself.

Catching yourself in the act of negative self-talk is a start. At one point, I reread an old journal from my early pain stages and I couldn't believe the harshness of the words I had written. The self-judgment was unbearable. The journals are proof that my internal monologue was a habit from well before the surgery that only grew in the face of adversity. No wonder the universe kept beating me up! I was setting the stage for a rough and tumble match every day whenever I looked in the mirror.

Stopping yourself is the next step. How can you flip the script? This is when the people who surround you are so important. The people who bring you down, verbally abuse you or mutter passive-aggressive comments about your vulnerabilities are not the ones you want to believe. Find the people who build you up, then listen and internalize what they say to you.

Dr. T. continually called me on my personal cruelty. By stopping and acknowledging my messages I was able to objectively consider what I was saying and decide if it was true or not. Slowly, but surely, I changed my internal dialogue to be more supportive and less judgmental, although by no means am I perfect at this, even today. Becoming a kinder, gentler companion to myself is an area of continuous and ongoing improvement.

Once you acknowledge that you're hurting yourself with your internal monologue, you can start catching yourself in the act, then counter those negative comments with more positive love notes. Just simple messages such as acknowledging your favorite body parts with kind thoughts or congratulating yourself for a job well-done will help. Eventually, with focused effort, the negative will be replaced by the positive. You'll start to love yourself again. From that place of acceptance, you can stand strong and create a life you love. When you calm the internal attacks, you'll be better equipped to handle the outside forces flying at you. It's more difficult to be a Resiliency Ninja when you're your own worst enemy.

Enough positive outside influences can help neutralize the negative self-talk and prevent you from believing the worst of your own messages.

Those who don't have positive forces around them have a harder time battling this kind of self-hatred. Even though hearing your mom say you're beautiful doesn't really count, it still sinks in and makes a dent to keep a person from hitting rock-bottom. If you're without that kind of unconditional love and reinforcement I'm sending you some right now. You do have gifts and areas of genius. Find them and own them with pride. Then find positive people who will recognize your worth and prop you up rather than tear you down. Reduce your time with the naysayers.

Another way I helped combat these personal attack ads was to make a list of my gifts so that I can tilt my life towards serving others through the lens of my talents. When I say something like, "Yep, that's my brilliance," people look at me sideways. But that's okay, because it feels good to be proud of my best bits, instead of pouring hatred on the areas where I lack.

The guy I mentioned who told me to be less confident? He went on to suggest I should tone down my happiness, because I won't find a man with that positive attitude. What this guy didn't realize is that it took years of healing to be able to say anything nice about myself, especially out loud. It proves that others can beat us down, but only if we let them.

I encourage you to a make a list of the attributes that make you feel proud of yourself, along with your talents and your areas of genius. You absolutely have them. So even if you're not happy with the size of your belly or the state of your career, you can look to this list and counterbalance your negative judgements with uplifting celebrations.

Self-adoration is a process, but when you get there it is really freeing, and actually kind of fun to not lather hate on yourself. Funny how hiccups in life bother you less when you're not in a state of constant internal battle.

You are your one constant companion for your life, so why not make this relationship the most peaceful, kindest, encouraging arrangement possible? A lifetime is a long time to have a cruel voice throwing punches at you from the inside, don't you think?

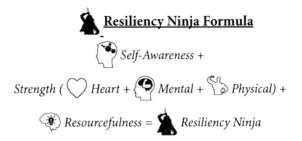

Resiliency Ninja Formula

Self-Awareness +

Strength (♡ Heart + Mental + Physical) +

Resourcefulness = Resiliency Ninja

 What are you saying to yourself? Are you in a state of constant internal battle running personal attack ads on yourself?

♡ *Be kind to yourself by recognizing and appreciating your areas of brilliance.*

 What are your talents and what are your downfalls (we all have them)?

 When you see yourself in the mirror, say out loud at least one positive compliment about yourself.

 Make a list of your best attributes so you can reference them to remind yourself to be nice to yourself.

 When a personal attack ad runs in your mind, physically stop, ask yourself if that is really the truth, and rewrite your internal dialogue to serve your best self.

29

Apples to Oranges that are Really Lemons

I'M A MASTER AT LOOKING joyful even when all hell is breaking loose in the background. Since I now know how easy it is to change the outside appearance of your inside emotional state by just changing the messages you're sharing, your body language and the expression on your face, it's really opened my eyes to the misaligned stories many professionals tell in public compared to what they live at home. Everyone has their own version of Whack-a-Mole.

Embracing this universal human struggle frees you from the constant comparisons to other people's supposed "perfect" image, even if you never get a glimpse behind their curtain. You can just assume that underneath all the bravado in the world there are a lot of hard knocks raining down on people.

Honor the fact that no one is perfect. No one is ON all the time.

Even knowing this, it's easy to unfairly compare yourself to another; and you don't have to look far to find it. It could be your neighbor who seems to have it all together while you're falling apart, a competitor who seems to have so many clients while you're still struggling, or a friend who paints a perfect image of her spouse while you're looking across the bed each night and wondering how you ended up with *that*.

My business has been up and down since the day I started. Even though on an annual basis the business has always done well, there are still slow months. Part of that is due to factors beyond my control, but other times it's because of limitations I put on myself. During these dips my instinct is to question my own worth and compare myself to others in similar businesses. On the surface we think we're comparing apples to apples, but that's impossible. We all have our own issues and no two businesses are the same.

There is one speaker-consultant I know who used to really get under my skin. She was quick to tell everyone how incredible her business was. Every time you speak to her she is either just finishing with a client or rushing off to one. Who has that many clients?

When you're frustrated with your own business and someone is gloating about their business, the natural instinct (unless you fight it) is to turn that judgment inward and feel like a failure by comparison.

I was guilty of this for a long time. When I was around this woman I could literally feel my confidence drain away. It's as if her business-is-perfect story was a trigger for my confidence to play hide-and-seek.

It turns out, however, that this woman's business-is-perfect mantra is her way of playing Whack-a-Mole. She's been caught in enough exaggerations of truth that I know she's struggling at times just like the rest of us. She's certainly mastered the knack of spinning her reality (a.k.a. lying) and managing her messages so that others don't see her truth behind the scenes. It's her defense mechanism. Once I realized this, two things happened. One, I started to feel empathy for her and prayed for her to find true success. Two, I completely released any sense of comparison – to her, and everyone else.

Even though I thought I was comparing apples to apples, I was actually comparing apples to oranges that were really lemons. It's unhealthy and counterproductive to let someone else dictate how you feel about yourself.

You could know a professional colleague – even a friend – for a lifetime and never really know the struggles that person's been through. Even now when I tell my pain story, most of my contacts are dumbfounded. They didn't realize the severity of what was happening behind closed doors. We all have masks.

There are women who put a smile on their face at work each day while they are secretly fearing for their safety each night because they are trapped in a cycle of domestic violence.

There are men who are one paycheck away from bankruptcy, and their family has no idea as they continue to shop for frivolous things on credit.

There's an entrepreneur who sleeps in his car because he's putting every penny into his business in faith that one day he will make it big.

There's the mom who is playing the role of the perfect wife and mother, yet on the inside feels estranged from her own identity and is about to hit her breaking point. She's convinced that if she steps on one more piece of Lego she's going to explode.

There's the dad who is sick of having to be strong and lead the family, and just wants to take a vacation and be vulnerable to his own fears and concerns about the future. We create our deepest connections with others when we get a glimpse at the true humanity behind their façade. Rarely do people expose their true challenges, for many reasons. Sometimes it's just not appropriate to let people outside of your circle of trust know the truth. Other times people hold back for fear of judgment or fear of losing their perfect image in the superficial circles they run in – heaven forbid.

I'm not suggesting we should all come clean publicly. You have a right to privacy, and some struggles are not for the public domain. That's okay. Choosing what you want to disclose is completely within your rights.

The value in recognizing that everyone has their own issues is that you can then release yourself from comparisons. You may not know what someone is going through, but you can trust that they are going through something difficult. Compassion, not comparison, is the answer.

Every time you compare yourself to someone else and judge yourself against their standards, nothing of value is created for you. The comparison drags you down and sucks up valuable energy that could better be spent getting your own house in order.

If you catch yourself wishing to be like someone else and ignoring your own gifts, let go of the instinct to compare. Imagine all the hardships they have had to fight to get where they are and empathize instead.

Never let someone's public image influence your internal perception of yourself.

Resiliency Ninja Formula

Self-Awareness +

Strength (♡ Heart + Mental + Physical) +

Resourcefulness = Resiliency Ninja

  Who are you comparing yourself to and why?

  Whose public image is influencing your personal perception of yourself?

What blanks do you fill in in someone's story to put them on a pedestal, even though you don't know the full truth?

Build compassion, not comparison by making a list of all the horrible things that could be going wrong behind closed doors.

What mask are you wearing publicly that is not authentic? What would happen if you removed it?

  Ask deeper questions when you're connecting with others to get a better sense of their struggles. You'll soon see the most perfect-looking people are not perfect at all.

30

The Spin Doctor

EARLIER I MENTIONED THAT I dated some not-so nice guys along the way. One was a con-man. He was an absolute master at twisting facts so much so that you believed anything he said. Even though deep down my gut knew something was off, I found myself sharing his wild tales and defending him when people cast shadows of doubt. My family was quick to his ways, but because he had presented facts in such a strategic way, what choice did I have but to believe him?

For example, he told me he owned a construction company that built custom homes. I'd hop in the passenger seat of his pickup truck and we'd go check out his various job sites mid-afternoon. He'd order the crew around and make comments about how this should be changed and that should be fixed. The crew would respond as if he actually had influence, so I just assumed he was the boss. It turns out, he didn't have anything to do with those job sites. He was just showing up, spewing bullshit and walking away. He didn't ever officially say, this is my crew and these are my builds, he just arranged the perception of facts so I would draw my own conclusions and feed into his fairy tale.

How ridiculous did I look just smiling along as he barked orders? Unfortunately, I wasn't the only girl he brought to the builds. It was his shtick…well, one of them.

In marketing or politics, they don't call it a lie, they call it spin. It's a widely-used manipulation to get people to see an event or issue from a biased perspective. Once you understand spin and how it works, you'll be less tempted to näively believe the exaggerated stories people tell us. Understanding how the spin doctor works is the cure for the common comparison.

In the past, a well-crafted marketing message could have had me reaching for my credit card to buy the latest magic fix. Now I know there is no magic fix for the most important goals in life. I recognize that a lot of marketing is just positioning and maneuvering facts, so they will resonate with the buyer. That understanding put me back in the driver's seat and made me less vulnerable to scams.

Keep in mind, not every story of success is spin. Not every builder who shows up on a job site is a scam artist. Sometimes people are in a really great place and are just telling the truth. Many products do work. There's a balance between naïve and cynical. Hone in on your spying senses. When your gut tells you something is off, something is usually off.

Let me walk you through some common, seemingly harmless spins to show you how a biased perception may influence your self-worth and what the marketing may really mean.

Spin Example 1: "Every event we've ever hosted has sold out."

Self-Comparison Judgment: "Really, wow, I scramble to get half of my desired attendees to come out to my event. I'm obviously horrible at running events."

Reality: The organizer changed the number of tickets they wanted to sell to represent the number of tickets they really sold. Voila, every event is a sellout.

Spin Example 2: "I'm an international speaker, sought-after around the globe."

Self-Comparison Judgment: "Really, wow, I only get speaking gigs within a three-hour radius. Obviously, I'm not very popular."

Reality: The speaker once did a speech, for a small honorarium, in another country to get a tax write-off for a family vacation.

Spin Example 3: "My book became a best seller on the first day."

Self-Comparison Judgment: "Really, wow. I have barely sold 30 books in the last 4 months."

Reality: The author organized an Amazon buy-blitz for an hour by having his family and friends buy his book all at the same time to push the book to a number one seller in a small category for one hour. Once it's hit the top for even a minute, you can call it a best seller. It doesn't need to stay at the top.

Spin Example 4: My kid is the superstar of his class, his club, and his sports team, and everything else he attempts to do.

Self-Comparison Judgment: "Wow, really, my kid only plays one sport in a rec league and is getting Bs in school. I must be a bad parent."

Reality: The kid is miserable because he's constantly being held to an impossible standard that he can't maintain and will peak in high school. He resents his parents for pushing him so hard and likely can't wait until he can escape, go to school, get drunk, smoke pot and drop out. (OK that may not exactly be his future, but hopefully you get the point.)

No one is perfect. Be mindful of how perceptions of reality can shift in a moment by only having partial facts or, worse, facts that are optimally arranged to tell a tale that can make you feel bad about yourself.

Once you recognize spin for what it is, it's not about being cynical; it's about weeding through the unrealistic perceptions half-seen through rose-colored glasses, to make informed interpretations that reflect reality.

Resiliency Ninja Formula

Self-Awareness +

Strength (Heart + Mental + Physical) +

Resourcefulness = Resiliency Ninja

Do you tend to take what people tell you at face value? Are you the person who falls for the latest marketing scheme?

Listen to your gut. If it tells you something is off, something is OFF. Do not ignore your intuition.

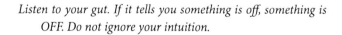

Before falling for a good pitch, analyze the story to check if it is factual or if it's spin. How has this tale been spun to make you feel uneasy about yourself?

Recognize spin when it's being spun to avoid falling for scams and feeling inadequate.

31

The Not-So-Jolly Green Giant

THE PROBLEM WITH COMPARISONS IS that more often than not, they result in that green monster, jealousy. There are few emotions that can make you feel less positive about yourself than when you put someone on a pedestal while you scrub the floors below them. Emotionally it is unproductive. It can even be destructive.

There were many times in the past when I was jealous of others. For a time, I was jealous of friends who were out having fun while I was stuck at home wallowing in grief.

There were a few times I felt envy when colleagues told me about new client projects they'd landed, which always felt unnatural because generally in business I am not a jealous person. In fact, I love to help others succeed and to hear of their success. I'm the one who encourages people to aim higher and go for it. At my core, I believe that a high tide raises all ships.

So, when I felt twinges of jealousy, it didn't make sense. I analyzed the emotion for what it was and dug deeper to figure out the root cause. Once I knew that, I could fix it.

Turns out my business momentum at any moment in time dictated how excited I was for others. If I was in a slump I was more vulnerable to comparisons, and its byproduct, jealousy. If I was on an upswing, I was genuinely happy for others to succeed.

I was oblivious to the pattern until one night when it showed up in a way that left me feeling disappointed in myself.

A good friend took the leap of faith from corporate America to try her hand at entrepreneurship. She launched her consulting practice and was off to the races. I was thrilled for her – completely supportive. All of a sudden, she had all these amazing contracts and the depth and width of her network were working in her favor. Kudos my friend, keep going.

Then the green jealousy giant arrived…

With years of pain and grief, I had reduced my networking functionality. That meant I had stuck close to my client base and my established network. Why not, it was working, even if I was frustrated with not expanding my reach as I had expected. There was a group of entrepreneurs I'd thought about breaking into, but there just wasn't a compelling enough reason to do so given I was focused on serving large corporations at the time. I think part of me felt resentful, not toward my friend, but toward the fact that this stupid surgery had restricted me from networking in this circle. I didn't even realize how much it disappointed me.

One night she texted me from the airport to share that she was flying to the east coast to speak to an audience of over 300 entrepreneurs. I suspect she was expecting an encouraging response from her usually supportive friend. Instead she got jealous Allie. I was like, "What? Are you ready for that? You know that audience size is really different and more difficult than smaller groups." Silence. Then, "Oh shit, now I'm nervous. Thanks a lot."

Who was I in that moment? What kind of a friend plants self-doubt into anyone else's mind the eve before she will be stepping on stage? It was so far misaligned with who I was authentically. I really dug deep to figure out what prompted this moment in time. The answer was simple: I was jealous.

Why was I jealous? Because she was out there busting her ass, drumming up new clients and I was feeling sorry for myself.

Several lessons came from this experience.

First, you can't have it both ways. I couldn't pride myself on running a successful company part-time and then resent that I wasn't working with clients five days a week like other people. It wasn't my current business model. Unless I wanted to change that, and at the time I didn't and couldn't, then comparing myself to fully-able consultants and speakers was not helpful. Now, thankfully, with my pain under control, I am able to embrace all the speaking gigs and coaching clients I can bring into my business!

Second, being confident and taking positive action to sort out personal issues is the cure for jealousy. The only reason I reacted in any way other than being absolutely supportive is because I had had a bad week. I didn't succeed in making all the sales calls I wanted, and I'd lost a $75,000 contract for reasons out of my control. I was frustrated with my own business and I projected my anger and sense of loss onto her. The two were not related, but the emotional lines were blurred. Remember the melting pot of emotions? They were all boiling together, and I was taking my frustrations out on the wrong person.

The third learning point was that when you screw up, apologize ASAP. When she got back from her big trip, we went for dinner and I came clean about where my head was the night I had let her down. I apologized profusely. There were a lot of tears on my part. She was nonchalant about it, but my behavior had ripped me apart. I was never going to let myself feel inferior and subsequently be unsupportive again.

Another person's success has absolutely no influence on your potential result. Even if they get a promotion and that means you didn't, there is still reason to celebrate. There are other, better-for-you jobs you can seek if that's really what you want, and in the meantime your co-worker will appreciate your enthusiastic support.

I can attest to the fact that action and confidence are the only cures for jealousy. Take care of yourself, stay aligned on your chosen path and I guarantee you'll care less about what others are doing. You won't have time to be envious.

Nowadays I'm pleased to say that jealousy has left my heart and my mind. All I offer now is celebration for others when they succeed and support when they need strengthening. In the middle if they ask for advice I'm happy to give it too. Goodness knows, I always have an opinion.

If you feel the twang of jealousy when you're scrolling Facebook or any other social media feed, STOP looking. It accomplishes nothing. Read a book, go for a walk, call a friend, do jumping jacks or a handstand or a cartwheel. Anything to switch gears because once you go down that jealousy rabbit-hole, pulling yourself out can be hard.

Jealousy is seeing in others something you know you are capable of achieving but haven't had the chance to yet. Now that you've seen it can be done, believe you can do it too and take your turn. Figure out how to do your own version of what you perceive their success to be. Jealousy will be a thing of the past for you too.

Resiliency Ninja Formula

Self-Awareness +

Strength (♡ Heart + Mental + Physical) +

Resourcefulness = Resiliency Ninja

 What triggers jealousy in you?

 What are you seeing in others that you wish you could accomplish for yourself? How can you make that a reality?

Who has or currently does inspire jealousy in you? Make a list of those people and the qualities you wish you had.

What actions can you take to focus on your own success rather than being jealous of what others are doing?

 How do you respond to people when you are jealous? Do you need to make amends for any bad behavior?

 Intellectually can you see what you wish you were doing reflected in the other person's actions?

 Make a list of positive distractions that you can use when you feel jealousy rear its head.

32

Musical Chairs, Who's Out?

CALL IT JEALOUSY OR COMPETITIVENESS, some people step on others as they rise to the top. There is so much abundance in the world why bother?

Both men and women engage in this combative behavior, but in many ways, society has set women up to be especially prone to the ugly side of the competitive climb. Back in the day when women were just beginning to be accepted in professional environments, there were only one or two spots at the top that women could fill.

This gender prejudice launched a game of musical chairs. The ruthless women who pushed everyone else aside were the only ones left with a seat at the big boys' table. When the music stopped, the last chair would go to the woman who threw the most elbows and kicked her high-heeled feet hardest. It was an era fueled by a scarcity mentality. At the root of scarcity is fear. In this case, there was fear that a woman wouldn't make it to the top unless she was the first and only one there.

I'm inspired by a genuine society where men and women can truly feel supported by each other. We need to stop pulling chairs away when the music stops. Instead we must start adding more chairs to the mix, to invite more people of both genders and various backgrounds to join a bigger table of success.

Thankfully, these days there is so much room at the top you can claim your seat at whatever table motivates you. You don't need the old boys' network anymore; you can create your own table.

It's so disappointing to hear stories of how professionals climb the ladder by stepping on others. If you have drama in your life, it's because you allow it. Each person has the choice to engage in drama and gossip or to be supportive of the underdog, even when they are under attack. When the negative chit-chat starts about someone else, just shut it down. Don't engage. It's so empowering to stop gossip.

We can also help each other. Earlier this year I attended a Global Sisterhood Circle founded by Nisha Moodley, (www.NishaMoodley.com). It's a worldwide movement where women take a pledge to support and honor each others' journey. I think men could benefit from the same kind of commitment.

Nisha's pledge is such a powerful manifesto that I asked her if I can share it with you here, and she graciously agreed. If you feel inspired, please sign the pledge and live it. Share it with others in your circle of influence to help spread the message.

www.SisterhoodDay.com

SISTERHOOD MANIFESTO

I will root for your success and joy, and see your wins as my own.

When I am jealous or envious, I will seek to access gratitude for the inspiration you offer, remembering that there is enough for everyone.

I will see your innate beauty, brilliance, power and capability, even when you can't see it in yourself. I will reflect it back to you when you need reminding.

I will listen to your desires and encourage your courage.

Sisterhood supports sovereignty. I will not attempt to fix you because you are not broken. Instead, I will see your wholeness and support you from the understanding that you are wise and capable. You've got this, and we've got you.

I will put my ear to your heart and listen carefully when I am with you, even if my mind is noisy. Hearing you will be part of my spiritual practice.

I will seek to stay present and grounded when you are expressing uncomfortable emotions. I will ask how I can support you.

I will stand in the truth that vulnerability is a sign of strength.

I will not share your secrets or speak badly of you to others.

I will recognize that the things I judge in you are showing me the places I hold a lack of compassion, and are access points to deeper healing within me.

I will honor our friendship as valuable, no less than the other relationships in my life.

I will seek to make time for you, even when I think I am too busy.

When you share things about your life, I will not make them about me or my life. We are each on our own journey.

As we move through different stages of our life, I will appreciate the unique gifts you bring to our relationship.

I will not claim any ownership over you, and will seek to celebrate new friendships and relationships in your life.

I will honor that our relationship may change over time, and regardless of how much we're communicating, I will wish you well.

If I am upset with you, I will be accountable for my own feelings, and will recognize that my emotional triggers are access points to self-love.

I will constantly deepen in love and compassion towards myself, and invite you to do the same.

Instead of closing my heart to you when I am upset, I will open my heart, even when it's hard.

I will tend to my own self-care and create the space I need for myself.

I will communicate my needs and desires without attachment to you fulfilling them.

If I am used to struggling in silence, I will practice reaching out in the spirit of not being sad alone. I will trust that this is not a burden to you, but rather a gift for all of humanity. I will allow sisterhood to be my salve, and will invite you to do the same.

I will take responsibility for my own life, asking for support when I need it but not holding expectations of you. I will give both of us room to make mistakes, and be messy and imperfect.

If I am fearful of connecting with women, I will not turn that fear into a judgment of all women.

I will honor that there are many ways to express as a woman. I will celebrate your unique expression.

I will honor that we are all "real women", no matter what our shape or size.

I will not make your age, weight gain, weight loss, relationship status, fertility, sexuality, choice to have children or not, successes or struggles mean anything about you or me.

I will honor that girls are not less than women, and that all ages have great wisdom to bring to the world. Every age is beautiful and can be challenging.

I will have compassion for and speak kindly of all women and girls, and see all as my sisters.

I will have compassion for and speak kindly of men and boys. We are all having a human experience, finding our way.

I will stand beside my sisters and brothers, never against men, as we are all one.

I will be gentle with your heart, seeing you through eyes of love.

I will be gentle with the hearts of the people you love.

I will care.

As we gather in sisterhood, we come home.

Together, we weave a tapestry of love.

Our grandmothers conspired for this moment.

Global Sisterhood Day | © Nisha Moodley International 2016

Resiliency Ninja Formula

Self-Awareness +

Strength (Heart + Mental + Physical) +

Resourcefulness = Resiliency Ninja

 Are you playing musical chairs to climb to the top, or are you trying to build a bigger table?

 Do you fear that there is limited space at the top, and therefore you need to kick and claw and take out your competitors, so you can win?

 How can you encourage and support others to reach their full potential?

 Another person's success does not reduce your potential.

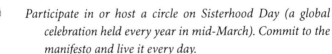 *Participate in or host a circle on Sisterhood Day (a global celebration held every year in mid-March). Commit to the manifesto and live it every day.*

33

Inspired Compassion

THE OPPOSING FORCE TO JUDGMENT, jealousy and competitiveness is compassion.

One Sunday, I was sitting in the pew at church watching the crowd, one-by-one, receive Holy Communion. It dawned on me, in a way that it never had before, that each one of those people has felt self-doubts, hurts, betrayals, grief and moments of joy and satisfaction as I have. Each has their own unique view of the world. Immediately I felt new empathy towards them because none of them got a free pass, either.

I'm not sure why I held this idea for so long that while I hurt, everyone else just coasted through life.

Intellectually I've always known that not to be true, but emotionally it had never sunk into my heart in such a profound way. Other people just seemed stronger than I was at dealing with their emotions.

We're all just doing the best we can, choosing the clothes and the attitude we put on each morning, and interacting with a set of people completely unique to our point of view. Seeing that so clearly was a mesmerizing experience.

That moment inspired a new kind of compassion in my heart.

My harsh judgments of others, and the unrealistic expectations for myself faded. I felt less ashamed of my imperfections and less alone in the frustration of navigating life. My heart felt like it needed to be less guarded.

Compassion eradicates jealousy when you emotionally accept that no one is immune to adversity. No business runs perfectly. No adult ever really feels like he or she has reached ideal circumstances.

It also made me more aware of how I treat people. I realized how much our words and actions can influence another person's day, for the better or for worse.

This realization makes me more aware of others' states of mind. When I notice someone else's energy seems sad or hurt or fearful, I'm more inclined to make an effort to bring a moment of joy to their life. It's an easy, inexpensive way to spread positive emotions in the world. Sometimes it may be a sincere smile or a compliment, and sometimes I'll buy them a drink. If it's appropriate, I might start a conversation that goes deeper much faster than your typical superficial busy-bee conversation. I feel honored when strangers tell me their troubles and I get to listen, without judgment, and hopefully share a message of hope in the ensuing conversation.

After I finished a keynote at a hotel in a major city in the United States, I went down to the lounge in the hotel for a glass of wine and a snack. If you've ever been in a Starwood Preferred Guest lounge, many times there are just a handful of people in the room, which makes it a delightful place to unwind away from the hustle of travel. It also makes it easy to unintentionally overhear others. That afternoon a lady and her boss were having a meeting – and it wasn't going well. He was quite a jerk in his approach to giving feedback. Short of me leaving, there was no way to not hear what he was saying to her. She held her own, but I could tell she was travelling on business and needed a friend. As they were wrapping up, I offered to buy them both a drink. He declined, she stayed. We spent the next couple hours talking about her work, her boss and her options to quit and get another job. I don't know her name, what company she works for or how it turned out, but I do know that at that moment a person needed an empathetic, non-judgmental ear and some compassion amidst a dark day. Why not be the person who can give it to them? By the time we were done, her spirits were lifted and she clearly appreciated the outreach.

Sure, I could have just minded my own business and turned up the volume on the TV in the lounge. I feel like society as a whole is so tuned into the noise of what's electronically fed to us that we miss the needs of the people – be they strangers or loved ones – around us. Being quiet, noticing the needs of others and offering a lending hand with no expectation for anything in return is one of the most satisfying contributions in life.

Granted, this habit of helping strangers thing can backfire.

I was in the hospital and noticed an elderly gentleman trying to steer himself in a wheelchair and looking lost. I said hello and asked if he needed help. It turns out he didn't know how to get to the room for his appointment. Upon further investigation, we realized it was on the other side of the hospital. Being somewhat of a regular in the hospital halls and trying to be a good Samaritan, I offered to roll him to the right room. We had a lovely chat along the way.

Suddenly, I heard a lady chasing after her dad. I didn't realize she meant the man I was wheeling. It was a bit startling when she ran up beside us, panicked because she had lost her dad. Apparently, she had been in line to grab a coffee when he and I met. We had a good laugh about my "kidnapping" her dad.

Winston reminds me every day to be compassionate toward people. He just loves meeting people. When Mom and Winston would take me to my appointments at the hospitals in Toronto, they would sit outside the front doors for hours greeting people and putting smiles on strangers' faces. Dogs can sense negative energy and will stay away accordingly, but beyond getting a sense that someone doesn't like dogs or may have a mean heart, dogs have no judgment. They love people of all races and sizes. It's beautiful to see.

Adopting a compassion-first approach to challenges gives you a better lens through which to view problems. Choosing to interpret the intent behind another person's actions as being well-intentioned can influence your response positively. Even if they aren't well-intentioned, it makes it easier to move on with your life after someone offended you. If you assume everyone is just doing their best to navigate their lives, then you'll come from a place of forgiveness and encouragement when someone cuts you off on the road, misses a deadline or makes a mistake. If your assumptions spring from a darker, more pessimistic perspective you'll be more guarded and faster to react harshly when someone crosses your path in an unfavorable way. You can choose to see situations through the most optimistic light.

Resiliency Ninja Formula

Self-Awareness +

Strength (Heart + Mental + Physical) +

Resourcefulness = Resiliency Ninja

 Do you have compassion for the struggles others face, or do you feel that others easily skate through life?

 When you're walking in society, look into the faces of the people who pass you. Are they joyful or do they feel sad or lonely? Is there something small you could do to let them know you see them, and help them understand they aren't alone in their sorrow?

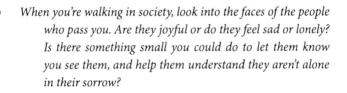

Compassion and love trump every negative emotion.

When you find someone else's actions irritating, can you find a way to feel compassion for them instead of judging them?

34

Expect Miracles, Strategize Solutions

So, IF WE ACCEPT THAT adversity, obstacles and stress are part of life what are we going to do about them? When I realized my pain was permanent, my instinct was to find a cure. I was desperate. I tried every snake oil I could find and begged and pleaded with health-care professionals to make the pain disappear. No number of tears would change the fact that a miraculous cure was not in my hands and it wasn't in the doctors' offerings either. I needed to leave the possibility of a miracle to my faith. I knew I had to start dealing with the aspects of this adversity that were within my control.

All that time I spent desperately searching for a magic bullet was pointless. It's like trying to make a con artist undo the damage he's done; it's not possible. He won't feel guilt, and he's probably already spent your money. The only thing you can do is to set your sights on the present moment and decide how you will shape your future.

Sure, hope and pray for a miracle, even expect it will eventually happen, but while the universe is working on that, pursue solutions that are within your control.

Solutions can be strategized, miracles cannot.

Wallowing in my pain story sucked away my sense of hope. It took a long time to realize what I could and could not control. It's normal to feel hopeless when your adversities are stacking up around you.

You need to shift your thinking. Focus on the tangible consequences from your adversity. Tilting your focus can turn hopelessness into hopefulness. Take small steps to succeed by creating solutions for the aspects of your adversity that you can influence.

Your attitude, your actions and the story you tell yourself and others are all within your control.

Fixing other people, making problems disappear and reversing time are not within your control. It was easy to blame my chronic pain for holding me back professionally and socially. That thinking was misleading; it kept me stuck because my blame was misplaced. While the nerve pain was the overarching cause, it was actually the results of the pain that caused my real limitations. The fallout, not the adversity, threw my life off-kilter.

From each adversity stems a whole series of issues or obstacles that you can deal with even if the root misfortune never goes away. In most cases, time will heal or lessen the hurt, but your life will never go back to normal again. Spending all your time wishing for something you can't make happen relinquishes your authority over the situation.

Acceptance is the most powerful "snake oil miracle drug" I have ever found.

Think about how some people with gluten intolerance say that the pain is not worth the pasta. Since they love pasta, their workaround is to use gluten-free noodles, cauliflower or another safe substitute in their favorite recipes. That's a workaround. Not perfect, but it's definitely better than giving up pasta because of their allergy.

Here's my Stay Strong framework for finding ways to power through when life sucks. I'll summarize it and then explain it more deeply.

The Resiliency Ninja's Stay Strong Framework:

1. List your challenges. Determine if they are a stress, obstacle or adversity.
2. Identify all the specific by-products that result from the stress and adversities you've listed.
3. Create workarounds for each of these resulting obstacles.
4. Adjust your tactics and notice arising by-products, until you've minimized the accumulated impact of your adversities.

To apply this formula to your circumstances, make a list of everything that is making your life hard: caring for aging parents, going through a divorce, suffering from pain or grief, dealing with financial troubles, and so on. Write down all of your adversities, obstacles and sources of stress. You can refer to your original list that we created in Chapter #14: *Turning*

Sticks into Sinkholes.

Next, let's break down each adversity into smaller, more manageable consequences that you can overcome. Basically, we want to identify all the obstacles that are caused by your adversities because obstacles we can tackle. Whatever your overarching adversities, each likely creates several derivative problems that interrupt your day-to-day life. Make a list of those secondary effects, and you can begin finding solutions.

The more thorough you are in identifying all the specific side effects of your adversities, the more effectively you can take control. Your list of secondary effects, a.k.a. obstacles, may be very long. The examples below are just a fraction of my own by-products list.

To get you started, here is a partial list of the obstacles that were caused by my chronic nerve pain.

- Sitting up straight was extremely painful.
- Driving for longer than an hour was excruciating.
- High-intensity activities such as presenting for a client would knock me out for a couple of days.
- Walking Winston regularly wasn't an option.
- I was experiencing constant exhaustion from fighting the pain.

Accepting that my pain wasn't reversible became a lot easier when I turned my attention to the secondary issues of the pain. Now instead of dealing with a huge, unmanageable sinkhole, I had a bunch of little sticks that, with some creativity, could easily be moved out of the way. (In the next chapter, I'll show you how.)

If it seems like there is no way to conquer each of these fallout effects, then you haven't yet broken down the adversity to a sufficiently granular level to enable you to start strategizing ways to overcome your obstacles.

For example, grief is an overwhelming emotion. At first, I had a hard time breaking down the devastation into manageable by-products. Eventually I analyzed a typical day for me, writing out everything that was hard to do because of the grief. Once I identified those individual problems, I could start to implement solutions in small doses.

Getting out of bed in the morning was one of my biggest challenges. My solution was to create reasons to get out of bed. I accepted that getting vertical equated to superstar status, and I aimed at making that my minimum achievement each day. I expected myself to work for an hour, after which I gave myself permission to go back to bed again.

Then I pushed myself even more. I booked client meetings in the morning and committed to deadlines that required my focused energy. This forced me to get moving and stop letting the days pass me by, lying in bed wallowing in grief.

Putting your adversities and their by-products into black and white can reduce your anxiety level, release your feelings of being overwhelmed, and put you back in control.

Resiliency Ninja Formula

Self-Awareness +

Strength (Heart + Mental + Physical) +

Resourcefulness = Resiliency Ninja

Are you focusing your energy on trying to manufacture a miracle that is out of your control?

What are the physical limitations placed on you by your adversities?

Chances are you can't change your adversity; you can only control your response to it. Know exactly what you can and cannot control.

Let go of longing for the way things were. In time, your heart will heal and you will find your new normal.

My Stay Strong Framework
1. List your overarching adversities, obstacles and stressors.
2. Identify all the by-products that result from these issues.
3. Create workarounds for each by-product.
4. Adjust until you've minimized the impact of your adversities.

35

Powering Through in Action

MY STAY STRONG FRAMEWORK CAN change your life. To demonstrate how effective it can be, I will break down my by-products list and show you how I created workarounds for each obstacle, so that chronic nerve pain didn't continue to take over my life. I did a similar exercise for all my other adversities as well.

For example, when I had two casts on my arms at the same time after the curling accident, I had to figure out how to keep producing my *Getting Connected* articles for the newspaper and use my computer for general work. I used a speech-to-text service, and fixed its errors using a keyboard that split in the middle so its angle was at a better fit for my wrists. If I had just sat back and waited until the casts came off, my career momentum would have stalled.

To make this an effective exercise, let go of your "This is how I've always done it" thoughts. I didn't write articles from my bed until I needed to write in a reclined position. If I had held myself to a standard that said I needed to work at a proper desk, I wouldn't have written very much over the last decade.

Here's how I worked through the by-products of my chronic nerve pain.

Couldn't sit:
Sitting is easy to take for granted. When I speak in front of an audience I can stand up, but the work I do to prepare for a speech and make calls for sales is generally done while seated at a computer.

So, if sitting wasn't comfortable, I asked myself what was. The pain was there no matter what, but it was less intense when I would lay back in a reclined position. So, I set up shop in my bed and bought a big comfy, burgundy leather recliner chair for my office. Most of my typing was done from a relatively comfortable reclined position rather than sitting at a traditional desk. Even today I have a couch in my office so that when the pain spikes, I can go horizontal to alleviate the pain while I keep thinking and working.

My issues about sitting also meant I had to choose my business and social activities more carefully. For instance, I love going to movies, so you can imagine how happy I am that my local theatre has added reclining seats. Before that I sat on the aisle and wiggled around a lot because of the pain. Social gatherings where I could stand and lean were more appealing than sit-down dinners. I was even happier when I could get comfy on a couch and just chat with friends without feeling I had to sit straight and be "on."

The first time I went to an awards' ceremony (a.k.a. long, boring event that requires you to sit still and straight-up) post-surgery, I snuck out in tears mid-way, and collapsed the second I got home. Eventually I learned to get up and mingle rather than sit the whole time. For long presentations, I often stand at the back of the room or excuse myself early.

The adjustments helped me feel better, but were subtle enough that others wouldn't notice and if they did, why would it matter? I still practice these workarounds today. Interestingly, I've found the more positively engaged I am in an activity, the more I'm able to ignore or repress my pain.

I also engage in the mental practice of accepting and dissipating pain. Basically, when pain spikes, I have a conversation with it (sounds weird, I know), say hello, welcome its existence then tell it to settle down and go away. Usually within several minutes I can drop the surge down the pain scale.

Couldn't drive long distances:

During my decade of hell, most of my speaking events, training gigs and doctors' appointments were at least a two-hour drive from my home. If I caught heavy traffic, those drives could easily last three to five hours. It became clear on a few occasions that it just wasn't safe to drive myself as the pain would spike while I was navigating traffic.

I removed this obstacle by having Mom drive me instead. So began the family road trips that remain some of my favorite memories from my worst pain years. Winston would be secured in his car seat in the back and just loved our adventures.

Most trips Mom drove me right to the front door for the client event, like my own private chauffeur. Then the two of them spent the day seeing the sights. Winston loved meeting people in the streets and parks. Of course, the best part of his day, and mine, was when I came through the doors to head home. He would go wild with enthusiasm. After a quick snuggle, he'd go into his travel case and get buckled into the back seat and I'd recline in the passenger seat while Mom drove us home. It was a great solution because I arrived at client engagements more refreshed, and it was a safer trip home than if I'd driven myself.

Of course, not everyone has a mom who will play chauffeur, and sometimes even Mom was busy. On occasion, I would hire a student to drive me. They got a trip to the big city and a few extra bucks in their pocket, and I didn't have to risk pain striking me at an unsafe time. Taking a train was sometimes an option, although the continual rocking of the car on the tracks usually intensified the pain.

If for whatever reason I had to drive myself, I would make several stops along the way or stay an extra night in a hotel to break up the trip. There are always workarounds!

Recovery needed after high-intensity activities:

Intense activity increased the severity of my pain. Once this pattern became obvious I looked at it objectively to figure out how to work around these obstacles. There was no doubt, for instance, that working full-time was no longer an option. That meant I couldn't jam my days full anymore and book multiple extreme activities in a week. Instead, I would book active events accordingly so they were followed by a day or two (or more) of rest or light activity.

Chunking my schedule gave me more control over my pain spikes. It also inspired me to make better decisions about what commitments and invitations to accept. For example, I would plan all my errands in a time block, my column writing in another and my recovery time in another.

Knowing that I could follow a heavy work day with rest days allowed me to power through at an important time. I could focus on my client's needs and shut out my personal pain because I knew that I'd soon be able to collapse and recover. Without that hope of a reprieve, I would have just given up.

One time I booked three client gigs in three days—with travel. It was hell, but the money was good and I was excited about sharing with all three audiences. The only way I got through this hectic schedule was knowing that on days four and five I would be at home in my bed, with no outside expectations.

Couldn't walk Winston daily:

Given that there were nights I would collapse in pain, sorrow or frustration, the idea of walking a dog daily was a bit of a conundrum. He needed exercise and he needed relief. Living in a high-rise, I couldn't just let him out the back door.

The day after I brought Winston home and took him to the vet, I explained my situation. He recommended training him to go on puppy-pads and outside. I made him his own indoor doghouse for a bathroom in emergencies and it worked perfectly. Being a small dog, he could get a lot of exercise indoors just with me throwing toys and wrestling with him on the floor.

To get Winston some fresh air and socialization with other dogs, I hired Dogzmopolitan, a dog-walking team who love him as much as I do. They take him on puppy adventures every day, even still, which alleviates some of the guilt I feel about not taking him for more walks. I know dogs thrive on routine, but Winston is understanding and goes with the flow.

Some may say he has a spoiled life, and I'm okay with that. He brings such joy into my world that I would do anything to keep him happy and healthy even when I'm feeling down.

Constant state of exhaustion:

Chronic pain is notorious for interrupting your sleep. But you can't heal without proper sleep. It's a vicious Catch-22. Interrupted sleep magnifies every problem.

I have found some strategies that help me get a better night's sleep. Now, thankfully, instead of having to sleep over 12 hours a night plus naps and still feel exhausted, I can feel refreshed with six to eight hours of quality sleep (plus a nap). I went to a sleep clinic that was very helpful and have implemented some other strategies such as creating an effective bedtime routine. If your sleep is interrupted, please talk to your health-care professional to find a solution. Getting a good night's sleep is the first task I'd put in your to-do circle every day until you figure out what works for you.

After three months of sleeping properly, I lowered my pain medications. The pain continued to lose intensity as my sleep improved. As I lowered my pain meds my sleep continued to improve, and so did my pain levels. The cycle just kept repeating itself. I believe that fixing my sleep was a turning point to give me back a full, active life. It's not that the pain is gone; it's that I'm more rested and stronger, making me better equipped to deal with it.

I HOPE THIS GLIMPSE INTO my strategic workaround plan helps you understand the power of the Stay Strong Framework. By tackling the offshoots of adversities head-on, one by one, you can overcome helplessness and despair and put your body, your mind and your life back on track.

Do you see how trapped I felt when I was only focused on fixing my pain? Once I identified the side effects of the pain and tackled each issue separately, I felt empowered and became more successful.

This is just a small part of the changes I made to take control and power through during life's punches. Your solutions, clearly, will be different. But being resourceful and creative will inspire small changes that add up to big wins. Too many people make excuses and focus on trying to make their biggest problems disappear. It's better to accept that the big adversities aren't going away. Breaking down the overwhelming challenges into smaller, more manageable issues helps you strike back against life's toughest blows.

Your workarounds are entirely within your control. Get creative.

I spent a lot of time working out my solutions. It's not that I woke up one day and said, "Gee, driving to Toronto hurts like hell, I should ask Mom to drive me." In the thick of things, the answers aren't always obvious.

Sometimes it's helpful to brainstorm ideas with trusted family, friends or advisors. They may see solutions from new angles and help you get unstuck. Together you can find new ways to overcome challenges. Breaking your big problem into smaller ones enables you to ask people for help to create specific solutions – and not asking them to manufacture miracles by making your big problems go away.

If you involve others in your brainstorming, don't let the conversation evolve into a pity-party. There is no value in enlisting someone else's help just to give you an opportunity to complain about how unfair your situation is. No one wants to listen to you sounding like a victim.

I hope that doing this flip of focus, which involves drilling down to solve the elements within your control, will be as transformational for you as it was for me. It's the only way I managed to stay in business through my decade of hell. If you carried out only this one exercise, you would still be well on your way to becoming a Resiliency Ninja.

Resiliency Ninja Formula

Self-Awareness +

Strength (Heart + Mental + Physical) +

Resourcefulness = Resiliency Ninja

 Can you break down your adversities even more to ensure you are dealing with the most fundamental by-products of your issues?

 Visit a health-care provider or sleep clinic to fix your sleep problems. If you don't feel refreshed after sleeping at night, please get help.

 Do not allow your discussions to evolve into a pity-party, where you feel sorry for yourself and wish for a magic wand to make your adversity disappear. It's not within your control to make those things happen.

 Give yourself permission to seek qualified help. It's not a sign of weakness, but a sign of smart strength.

 Engage trusted advisors in your Stay Strong Framework brainstorming exercise. They may be able to see new ways to work around your obstacles.

Get creative in your workarounds. The Stay Strong framework is the answer to being resilient when life sucks.

Enlist those closest to you, family members, friends and mentors to help in creative areas. Asking for help is not a weakness.

36

The Busy Badge of Honor

THERE'S A REAL ESTATE AGENT in town who constantly proclaims how busy he is. It's his badge of honor. When a friend of mine was his client, she constantly felt awkward calling him. She thought she was intruding on his busy day. The same guy frustrates his friends because he won't relax and enjoy the moment. He's always talking about his busy to-do list.

Why is busy the typical answer to, "How are you?" It's like people are proud to pronounce their busy-ness. If they don't appear crazy busy they seem to think something is wrong, and they are letting society down.

I think it should be the other way around.

Think of Virgin founder Sir Richard Branson, who controls hundreds of companies. He has billions of dollars under his guidance and always seems to be doing something profound. If anyone deserves to say he's busy all the time, it would be him. But I doubt he does. A proclamation of being busy is not sharing anything of value. It's a cop-out.

The more successful someone is, I find the less they play up their busy-ness.

Imagine a busy-busy bee. Just flying around, flapping its wings like crazy so it doesn't plummet to the ground. Buzzing from one flower to another, then coming back to the hive to do whatever it is bees do before rushing out again. Why would you want to be a busy-busy bee? It's so devaluing. You're not a bee, you're a human. You get to make choices with your time.

Want to become a Resiliency Ninja? Delete the word busy from your vocabulary. When someone asks how you are doing, you can answer any way you want, except you can no longer say you are busy. You aren't. Instead, you prioritize the activities with which you fill your days and nights. Being busy doesn't set you apart, above or below others. It's inconsequential in adding value to your reputation, but it could negatively impact how others perceive you.

Wearing the busy-bee badge of honor is basically showing the world that you aren't making good choices with your time—and that you're not available for any new opportunities that could be coming your way. It sends the message that you don't care enough about yourself to choose activities that make you feel grounded and content. It also is a passive excuse as to why the right things aren't getting done. After all, you're so busy, how could you expect to have a successful career, as well as take care of yourself, be a good parent AND have a successful romantic life and ... and .... and .... and...?

Continually reinforcing how busy-busy you are also exaggerates the circumstances around your adversities. Talk about adding another layer to hardships in your life. Not only do you have to go through hell, but you're telling yourself and everyone who will listen that you're too busy to deal with it.

See the problem?

If you are one of these busy-busy bees, let's figure out why. What does being so busy accomplish for you? Is it martyrdom? Are you hoping people will finally recognize how much you sacrifice for them? Is it because being busy with everyone else's stuff means you don't have time to be quiet and figure out your own?

For a long time, I kept my mind either busy-busy or numb, so I wouldn't have to acknowledge my emotions. There was no in-between. "Deflect and distract" was my way of life, so I understand the appeal of being extra busy. How can you hurt if you just keep ploughing through, ignoring messy reality? Making excuses that you're too busy to care for yourself is an avoidance technique. Eventually it catches up with you. The universe, as it did me, will find a way to slow you. Busy allows you to skim over all the bad stuff so it takes guts to include quiet downtime in your schedule.

How can you add "self-care" time into your already overloaded calendar? You have to make the time. If you have a spouse, kids, pets, work and maybe a volunteer commitment which you truly care about, and I was to tell you to delete one of those responsibilities from your calendar, would you? Of course you wouldn't. You've chosen to make time for all those commitments. So why do you automatically delete the one category that is the most important common denominator in all those activities: YOURSELF?

People make time for what they prioritize, or for what others prioritize for them. You need to be able to make this decision for yourself and automatically include you in your productivity efforts. We'll talk about how to fit all your top priorities into a day in an upcoming chapter.

Sure, you can fill your days, but fill them on your terms and resist the unhealthy busy-is-best culture. Busy is not best. It's bullshit.

Resiliency Ninja Formula

Self-Awareness +

Strength (Heart + Mental + Physical) +

Resourcefulness = Resiliency Ninja

 Do you treat being busy as a badge of honor? Why?

 What does being busy accomplish for you? Does it allow you to avoid handling important issues?

 Prioritize time for self-care. Don't delete "you" out of your to-do circle.

 When you slow down, do you feel emotions you wish you could avoid?

Delete the word "busy" from your vocabulary. You are no longer busy: you make choices and prioritize what fills your 24 hours of each day.

37

Really? Well, Pace This

THERE'S NOTHING WRONG WITH TAKING more time for yourself. But you have to do it on your own terms. Your body, your thoughts and your language all need to be congruent for you to heal and be your best self – even though the world often tries to impose its own unwelcome standards on you.

There's a flip side to busy which is not busy at all. It's being bored out of your mind, with nothing of value to do, just sitting and wallowing in your own personal-hell-kind-of-a-day. When true adversity strikes, such as death, divorce or major injury, you need downtime to heal emotionally and physically, which can be very frustrating when you have a long list of tasks that need to be done. When life throws you lemons, don't judge yourself for taking time away from your typically hectic pace. Resist the cult of busy and do what you have to, without guilt or shame.

When the shit hits the fan and the blades are spinning on high, press pause and assess the situation objectively. Does this problem require all your focus right now, or can you maintain your regular pace and deal with it after hours? If you can't keep going, then take the time to sink into the circumstances around you. Leaning in with intent will get you back to full speed faster.

For me, learning how to take the downtime I needed without the self-judgments that went with it involved a steep learning curve.

The health-care system is designed to hold you back. The doctors don't see enough patients pushing through the pain and so they expect defeat. Thriving in the face of major pain is the exception, not the rule. I hope to change that through my work helping people become Resiliency Ninjas.

At the pain centre the doctors have a clear protocol. At the heart of their process is the expectation that you will ultimately see a pain therapist or a psychologist specializing in acquired pain.

I saw a few different professionals before I found Dr. T. He became my confidant on the journey of neuropathic pain, and all the ups and downs that have gone into creating the post-surgery life I now enjoy. Unfortunately, one of the therapists I met before him was not a good fit for me. She was a very mild-mannered, soft-spoken therapist, and as you may have gathered by now, I do not share those characteristics.

Her main goal was to get me into group sessions with other chronic pain patients. That just didn't work for me. I left the group angrier than when I arrived—mainly because everyone in the room had let their pain become their identity. Remember the ice cube that became the snowman?

Even though I refused to continue with the group, I still had appointments with this doctor. Every week she would drone on and on about me having to learn to "pace" myself. For whatever reason the word "pace" triggered me. It made me feel defeated. I had never paced myself in my life. I just did whatever it took to get the job done, and I had fun doing it.

She refused to stop using the word, and I got angrier and angrier. One day I just exploded and said, "You want me to pace? Really? Well, pace this." I left in tears, never to return.

It later became clearer to me that "pacing" is typical pain language; every doctor would give me the same suggestion. Every time I hear the word pace, I imagine a pace-car in a race. It starts slowly, holding everyone back, then builds and as soon as it gets momentum it retreats off the track. The pace car never gets to realize its full potential. It watches as everyone else speed by.

That's why I hate being told to pace my life. I don't want to pull off the track and let everyone go by. I want to stay in the race that I choose to live, even with a few broken parts.

To overcome this cringe, I replaced the word "pace" with "control." At some point along my medical journey I asked a doctor to write this wording preference in my medical file, ensuring no one would ever tell me to "pace" again. Even so, one day an arrogant resident started to lecture me on the need to pace and I lost it on him.

The message I prefer is that I need to control my schedule. That puts me in the driver's seat on this journey. Instead of saying no to an event because my body is feeling weak, I feel more empowered declining an event because I chose to do something else: recoup.

It was a small word change that made a huge impact on both my outlook and my acceptance of my own limitations.

What words are you using that make you feel defeated? How can you flip them?

Back in the day I would describe my pain in words such as "horrific," "traumatic" and "devastating". Not surprisingly, I would feel horrific, traumatized and devastated.

The language you use around all types of challenges will tell your brain how it's to interpret these problems. Your brain believes what you tell it. So, if you choose defeatist words to describe a situation, you will subconsciously act to prove your thoughts are right. That's why I dislike the word "busy". It tells the brain you're already at capacity – when chances are you're nowhere near it yet.

Good job, brain; bad job us for giving the brain the wrong stories to believe.

I often catch my coaching clients using extreme phrases to describe a tough day. I'll read them back their words and confront the accuracy of their dramatic adjectives. Ultimately, they start laughing. Situations are rarely as bad as our words would suggest. When we use strong, defeatist language, stress intensifies. Shifting the words we use for better ones, for example pace to control, horrific to tough, busy to rocking it, is something you can do to become more adaptable to change. Flipping words to be more optimistic and supportive will make it easier to become a Resiliency Ninja.

Resiliency Ninja Formula

Self-Awareness +

Strength (Heart + Mental + Physical) +

Resourcefulness = Resiliency Ninja

 What defeatist words are you using to describe your adversities, obstacles and stressors?

 Flip your defeatist language to empower you to be a Resiliency Ninja.

 Your brain is brilliant. It will deliver based on the language you use to describe your circumstances.

 You don't have to buy into others' expectations and wording choices that lead to you feeling defeated or worse, a victim.

 In tough times, ask yourself: "Is this a true adversity that needs me to stop and heal fully right now, or can it wait until later?"

38

Owning Your No

GRETCHEN RUBIN, author of *The Happiness Project* and *Better than Before,* spoke at a conference I attended recently. Hearing her words was like suddenly having a lightbulb turned on, illuminating my whole life. She talked about the difference between people who reach goals or create new, positive habits and those who fail. One major influence is how you respond to internal or external motivations.

Based on her "Four Tendencies" framework, (four basic ways that people respond to internal and external expectations) it turns out that I am, without a doubt, an "Obliger." (The other possibilities are Upholder, Questioner and Rebel.) Being an Obliger means that if I have a client deadline, I'll make it. If a friend calls me and needs help, I'm in. An Obliger puts other people's expectations ahead of his/her own. That also means an Obliger is not as inspired to meet their own internally-driven goals. Where there is no external accountability, Obligers are less likely to achieve their own goals.

Hearing Gretchen speak for less than an hour completely shifted my perspective on my life. Now I understand why I will drop my expectations for myself to appease someone else's request. If I'm truly honoring my needs, I would say no, or at least move tasks for others to a more convenient time for me. (For more information about Gretchen's Four Tendencies visit www.gretchenrubin.com)

To control your schedule, you need to get good at saying no and choosing which activities you want to add into your calendar. That's easier said than done, of course, because there are so many conflicting priorities on your time, especially from outside sources like family, friends and work.

The funny thing is, as a business and communications professional I thought I had mastered saying "No." Then I took an inventory of the tasks in my to-do circle and found that the clear majority were items for others' benefit that did not directly create value for me or my business. Of course, the personal fulfillment that comes from helping others can be rewarding but helping others mustn't always work to the detriment of your own priority projects getting done.

Saying yes when you really want to say no causes resentment, which makes it nearly impossible to go from funk to fantastic (which we'll talk about in the next chapter). How can you be expected to change your vibe from resentment and obligation to enthusiasm and engagement when you're about to do something that you don't really want to do?

It's harder to say no when you don't have a clear understanding of when you want to say "Yes."

There's a saying in business that you are defined as much by what you say no to as by what you say yes to. When you learn to say no, there is a rush of self-worth that comes from setting boundaries with kindness and confidence.

Two reasons people have difficulty saying no include guilt and misplaced responsibility. Somewhere along the way we learned that we need to please everyone, and we forget to please ourselves.

If you say yes too often, you must figure out why. Who holds you to a standard that you don't need? Who are you worried about letting down? Where is the judgment that says you must do it all? Where does it come from and why do you allow yourself to buy into this belief?

There are times to say yes professionally. For that I have a framework I call the *Sweet Spot of Profitable Activity* that you can access in my book, From Business Cards to Business Relationships: Personal Branding and Profitable Networking Made Easy! (John Wiley & Sons Ltd. 2012) Knowing when to say yes will help you decide when to say no.

The same principles I outline in this business tool apply to making decisions personally too. It's just that life tends to be more fluid than a four-part worksheet allows. Essentially, if an invitation doesn't positively contribute to your life and you don't feel emotionally compelled to go, then you have the right to say no.

You are the only one responsible for your schedule. Whenever you allow someone else to make choices in your calendar, you relinquish control of your own life, ignoring your desires and needs. Don't let others dictate the activities you jam into your schedule because it's a major setback when you want to become a Resiliency Ninja.

Many people are uncomfortable saying no. No one likes to feel like they're letting others down. I can empathize.

The key to saying no is to do so succinctly. Never justify your decisions. Giving excuses just adds to the guilt. A simple, "Wow, thanks so much for the invitation, but unfortunately, I'm not available" is plenty of explanation. Try it and see how it feels. Don't overplay your disappointment at turning them down, or they'll keep asking.

If the conversation continues and they try to arm-wrestle you into doing something you don't want to do, then use my "Own Your No" formula:

Compliment + Onus + Reaffirm + Thank = No

Compliment them:
"I really appreciate how committed you are to the cause; the charity is lucky to have you."

Put the onus on you:
"Knowing everything I have on my plate, I can't take on another responsibility (event/activity). I wouldn't to do it justice (enjoy it/participate actively)."

Reaffirm:
"So, I need to decline the opportunity."

Thank:
"Thanks again for thinking of me. It means a lot coming from you."

It's that easy. You are firm, kind and fully within your right to choose.

Some say saying "No" is a complete sentence. It is. And I've found that most are not comfortable with that approach – on both the giving and the receiving end. The goal in saying no is not to burn a bridge or stall a relationship. Therefore, to have a sense of comfort for both parties, I believe there needs to be a softer approach that allows everyone to save face, thus, my formula.

There are times when you want to say no, but deep down you know you need to say yes. For example, I don't enjoy taking Mom to her doctors' appointments. Who would? Being surrounded by medical equipment, dredges up memories that suck.

Even so, I say yes because it's the right thing to do. Let's not forget she gave up her life to move in with me and take me to my appointments. Now I ask her to just let me know in advance, so I can book the times in my calendar. When I go, I bring my laptop or iPad and make the most of the time while I'm waiting. Whenever I am forced to say yes when I really wish I could say no, I do everything I can to make it a positive, productive experience.

Resiliency Ninja Formula

Self-Awareness +

Strength (Heart + Mental + Physical) +

Resourcefulness = Resiliency Ninja

     Do you find it difficult to say no? Who is controlling your schedule?

     Use the "Own Your No" formula:
Compliment + Onus + Reaffirm + Thank = No

39

From Funk to Fantastic

WHEN I WASN'T FEELING WELL for so long, I would often say yes to invitations when I wanted to say no. Often I would cancel at the last minute, or go to the event for a bit, be miserable and leave early. From a professional perspective, it's not good to be a no-show. From a friend's perspective, it's even worse.

The last straw for me was skipping a friend's New Year's Eve party. I remember the night like it was yesterday. I was feeling sorry for myself and didn't want to be around people. I figured no one would even notice I wasn't there. Doesn't that just sound like something a depressed person would say to downplay her own importance?

I found out the next day that my friend did notice and wasn't impressed by my no-show. I made a New Year's resolution that I wouldn't leave a friend hanging again. If I said I would attend, I would attend enthusiastically, at least for a bit. For the most part I have honored that resolution ever since.

You must own your "Yes" as much as you own your "No."

Saying yes to anything means you're saying no to something else. So, when you say yes, be prepared to engage in that activity 100 percent. Before my decade of pain, I usually said yes just because I was invited. Post-surgery I say yes because either I really want to go, or there is business value in going.

Keen self-awareness can help you anticipate better when you will and won't be up for an outing.

I'll say no when I know that my schedule is getting too overloaded, if I don't think I'll enjoy the activity, or if it won't serve a positive purpose. Life is too short to bother saying yes when we want to say no, don't you think?

Setting expectations in advance that I won't attend ensures no one feels let down. Obviously, getting sick or other important circumstances may prevent attendance every now and again. It's just better to make cancelling the exception, not the rule.

What happens if you said yes, but you feel awful and aren't in the mood to go?

How do you go to an event and not be a downer, even when your business is falling apart, you're feeling depressed or you just had a fight with your significant other? It's not easy, but it's absolutely doable. You need to find your own secret to go from funk to fantastic.

Make it a ritual as you enter an event that you completely shift gears. Park all your problems at the door. Just as you wouldn't drive your SUV into the restaurant, you need to leave your emotional baggage in the parking lot. To leave challenges behind takes conscious effort; otherwise, the most pressing issues of the day will stay with you and disrupt your positive interactions with others.

In my lowest days, I knew I had to shift my energy before walking into an event. I call it resetting my juju (that's the word I use to indicate a charismatic vibe). Too many times, if I didn't purposefully reset my mood, I found myself oversharing, being discouraging to others, or lacking authenticity. Unless I consciously left my problems behind, they would consume me—and I just couldn't fake a confident, positive juju.

Self-awareness makes this sort of control possible.

Just blocking challenges out of your mind won't get you ready to step into an office or event with confidence. You still need to figure out what will shift your juju from funk to fantastic.

There are so many ways to change your vibe; everyone is different.

Very loud music and dancing are my favorite vibe-changing techniques. It's amazing how powerful the perfect song with a strong beat can be when shifting your energy. Create a playlist of music on your phone or in your car that will make you smile on demand. In the next chapter we'll talk about some physical moves that can instantly shift you from low-vibe to high-vibe superstar, at least for long enough to power through when required.

Another way is to shift acknowledgement of your blessings to the forefront of your mind so that negative thoughts don't have a chance to take over your emotions. You have the power to choose to focus on the positive and send the bad stuff to the background.

To help facilitate this shift in perspective keep a notepad handy.

Have a list of all your blessings available on a moment's notice. Read the list and imagine the love and joy that comes from those beautiful memories, people or situations.

Before you go into an event or meeting, jot down a quick list of the problems that are weighing heavily on your mind. Do a quick calculation of the value of worrying and multiply that by zero. Worrying solves absolutely nothing.

If it assists you with the ritual of shifting your juju, fold up the paper with your troubles listed and leave it in the glove box of your car for the duration of the event. Commit that you won't give your problems another thought until you are back in the car and reopen the glove box.

If negative issues creep into your mind, visually take them and stuff them back into the glove box. By having a ceremonial safe place to park your troubles, you can give yourself permission to let go of your stress for the duration of the event.

Next, before going into the party, consider what would best relieve each of the challenges on your mind. For example, if money troubles are at the forefront, then perhaps landing a new client or finding a higher-paying job would have a positive impact on your circumstances. Instead of focusing on the adversity or obstacle, be optimistic that in the next room you could meet your perfect prospect or your ideal new boss. A better perspective means a better mindset – which makes it easier to be a Resiliency Ninja.

Resiliency Ninja Formula

Self-Awareness +

Strength (♡ Heart + Mental + Physical) +

Resourcefulness = Resiliency Ninja

 Create a ritual before you walk into an event or meeting to leave your worries behind and focus solely on who is in front of you.

 Write out your problems and put the list into your glove box or another ceremonial place to leave them until you are done your commitment.

 Write a list of your blessings and keep it with you all the time to restore your good mood.

 Create a playlist of motivating music that can shift your juju and play it before an event.

 Considering your list of problems, what resources do you need to solve them? Is there someone you may meet or an idea you may glean that you can focus on for each event you attend?

40

What Gives You Your Power?

CONFIDENCE IS A POWERFUL EMOTION. It enables you to keep going even when life sucks. Identifying what inspires confidence for you and what robs you of it can be the most important tools you have when you need to change a negative state at a moment's notice.

It's often the small things that will shift your juju – that *je ne sais quoi* that makes you look and feel like you can handle anything life throws your way. There's a little bounce in your step that says, "That's right, I've got this." The goal is to be able to get into that frame of mind whenever you want to or need to.

One of my favorite teachings from Tony Robbins is that you need to teach your most powerful self to show up on command, the same way you would train a dog to come when you call it.

I have such a line. When I say it with the right attitude and swagger, it immediately snaps me back into my most powerful, confident self. I say my phrase and automatically turn my thoughts to the present and future, ignoring the imperfect past. All my accomplishments come rushing to the forefront of my mind, fueling inspiration and purpose.

It's remarkable that just two words have the power to completely shape how I show up. Writing my words, which are simply, That's Right!", isn't enough. Without the right tone the phrase loses its oomph. I promise if you hear me speak at a conference about the ideas in this book, that I will share my magic juju-shifting words so you can hear the essence that is behind the words.

Another phrase I use a lot is FU-CHAAA. It's the sound of a ninja stealthily moving assailants out of his way with a karate-ish move. You can check out my Resiliency Ninja podcast and You Tube Channel (@

AllisonDGraham) to see the FU-CHAAA in action!

It doesn't matter what my phrase that pays is – what matters is yours. What can you do to anchor your most authentic, most powerful self? Develop a line, use an inside joke or bust a physical move that means optimism and joy, so that when you do that gesture or say those words you will instantly go from funk to fantastic.

How will you put yourself into your best possible mood on demand? Tony Robbins calls this your peak state, the strongest version of yourself and it's the best place from which to make decisions. At the Tony Robbins seminar I attended I noticed a lot of people thrust their fist into the air as their moved. I will sometimes thrust my fist out my sunroof when I'm about to go into a sales meeting or give a speech. (You'll notice I'm doing that on the cover of this book.)

I'm also a fan of the 'superstar' jump move from the 1999 movie Superstar, starring Molly Shannon. It's when she throws her arms up in the air and springs her legs into a forward-squat. (OK, the movie does it more justice than my explanation.) No judgment on this, whatever move works as your anchor to recall your best self, make it.

Another way to get into your best state before you show up somewhere is to be sure the clothes you're wearing match your desired mood. It's hard to be fierce (in a good way) when you're wearing yoga pants and an oversized hoodie. Throw on a power suit or a hot pair of jeans with a blazer and now you're talking. What you wear has the power to completely transform how you show up in the world.

Have you noticed there are some outfits that just drain you, and there are others that make you feel like a rock star? Knowing this, why do you wear the muted, baggy suit that makes you feel frumpy? You can't strike a superhero pose feeling frumpy. It's like setting yourself up to have a lackluster day.

One of my best friends for the last 15 years is great at noticing when I'm not in my peak state. She's very astute. We're the kind of friends who will say, "Let's grab a quick dinner," and then we'll be out for hours laughing and catching up. There's nothing brief about our visits.

Except for one night. I was completely out of sorts. My pain was severe. It was just after the string of deaths, and I felt like I had lost 10 rounds in the ring. As I arrived for dinner, she just looked at me and said, "Ah, Allie, this [pointing at me] just will not do. You're better than this." I was wearing shabby clothes. I had no make-up. My hair was tussled in a messy pony (and not the styled version that looks hot). Pain and agony were written all over my face.

She gave wise counsel. It was a reminder that even though I was going through hell at home, there was a time and a place to show the world I was exhausted from playing Whack-a-Mole – and our favorite restaurant in the city was not that place. She'd be the first to wallow with me if I asked her to do so in the privacy of her own home. Order takeout if you need an indoor evening; don't go to a hot spot that attracts the who's who of your community.

Shoes and other accessories like purses, jewelry, ties and watches may seem insignificant at first glance. Don't be fooled: those little afterthoughts have the power to transform outfits from okay to amazing. The more polished you look, the more confident you'll feel.

The extra height from a good pair of high-heels or the pizzazz of some sparkly bling makes me feel strong, confident and feminine. I don't know why, it just works, so I embrace the power of accessories.

Knowing heels are important to my presence on stage, it was a bit of a conundrum when I broke my big toe and had to keynote for an important client. The clunky air-cast didn't reflect my typical, confident look, and I walk around a lot when I'm presenting. So, just before I went on stage, I removed the clunky air cast and slipped into a pair of flats. They were better than drawing attention to my injury. Not because the audience wouldn't understand but because of the way hobbling around killed my juju. It hurt like hell, but I powered through and most people wouldn't even have known I was injured. Wearing flats on stage made me feel flat in comparison to the heels I normally wear. I pulled off that session, but I hope I don't have to do that again.

With my knee still tender from the torn MCL and the bone-on-bone arthritis in my big toe (yes, the same one that was broken), wearing heels comes at a cost. Therefore, I wear flats or short wedges on the way to an event and change when I am there to minimize pressure. I'll wear hot high heels for a media event, speaking engagement or photo shoot but will take them off as soon as I no longer have to be "on." It's another workaround that continues to serve me.

What do you do with this idea? Start by going through your closet and assigning a positive vibe rating to every article of clothing and accessory you own. Find the pieces that make you pop. Set them aside and wear them on any day you want to shift your juju or have an amazing day.

If you're having a bad day, put on some sparkle, a hot pair of shoes and jeans that fit just right. Voila, you'll feel like new again. Dressing in your best is one way to turn a lack-luster day into one that makes you feel on top of the world.

My friend, a very successful entrepreneur, says a good hair cut will turn around a bad sales day. When he wants to amp up his juju (FYI, he would never use that word) he goes for a hair cut and it resets his vibe.

As we've already covered, but it deserves repeating, the people around you will also influence your feelings of personal power. Are there people who support you in a way that shatters your excuses? Engage with them every chance you can. Are there people who make you feel inspired and ready to take on the world, while others leave you depleted? Recognize the difference by doing a gut check each time you finish an interaction with someone. Knowing whose energy charges you the best will tell you who to call anytime you want to shift into a positive mood.

What environments make you feel most confident, and how can you spend more time in those places? I love being at entrepreneur events when the vibe is "Dream big and take action." I go to those events every chance I get.

Resiliency Ninja Formula

Self-Awareness +

Strength (♡ Heart + ⊙ Mental + Physical) +

Resourcefulness = Resiliency Ninja

 When do you feel like your absolute best self? Who is with you, where are you, and what are you doing? How can you shape your life to include more of those positive influences?

 Create a short phrase, joke or physical action that can quickly shift your juju from funk to fantastic.

 Spend time in environments that support your most powerful, authentic self.

 What physical move can you do to anchor your most powerful, authentic self?

What clothing and accessories make you feel like you can accomplish anything? Rate all your clothes from frumpy to fierce. Choose what to wear accordingly.

41

Eminem, Belly Breaths and Rest

FROM 2010 TO 2013, my main source of nerve-pain relief was an ultrasound-guided nerve block that lasted about five days. In non-medical terms, the anesthesiologist freezes the area by inserting a needle into the canal that carries the nerve. My insertion point was in the crease between my upper hip bone and belly, typically a tickle zone, but this was no time to laugh. Thankfully, the doctors give you enough sedative to temporarily block feeling to that region, so the relief of the procedure outweighs the discomfort.

That was, until one day, when I showed up for a scheduled nerve block and there was no procedural room available with the necessary equipment and anesthetic. I was going on a trip the next day, so I was not leaving the hospital without a nerve block.

The doctor, his medical fellow and I discussed the options and ultimately decided to perform the procedure in a regular hospital room. The first attempt was aborted because I could not handle the pain. The insertion was worse than the serrated edge knife I had felt twisting into my body for five years, and I wimped out.

Then I took a minute to regroup. I turned to the only comfort I had at that moment, my iPad full of music. With my earbuds on full volume I blasted the heaviest Eminem songs I had so loudly I literally couldn't "hear" the pain. (This was no time for a pop ballad.) Don't get me wrong, I felt the pain. I knew the doctors were deep inside a nerve canal. My eyes were producing tears, a natural reaction to physical agony; however, I mentally survived letting the doctors finish. I drowned my pain sensors for the procedure, which thankfully lasted just a few songs, and came out the other end with a blessedly blocked nerve. The experience was hellish, but I now believe, without a doubt, that with the right mental strength and focus, the body can get through whatever you ask of it.

One secret to calming the body is in the breath. "Just breathe" is one of those pieces of advice, like "pace yourself," that makes my skin crawl. Obviously, I need to breathe; in fact, my body is doing that already.

It wasn't until I went to see a doctor of Ayurveda medicine, a body of knowledge originating in India, that I really understood how to take a breath that will actually calm the entire body.

Before I learned this trick, whenever I took a deep breath my lungs would inflate and my chest would expand as you'd expect. But I couldn't tap into the calming influence in times of anxiety or stress that gurus promised from deep breathing. In one minute, however, my Ayurvedic doctor taught me a simple trick to achieve a deep belly breath that does the most good.

The technique is to smile with the back of your tongue. It sounds weird, but it works. Basically, push the back of your tongue down and move the sides of your tongue slightly upwards (imagine where your tonsils were) like the tongue is smiling at your throat. The first time I did this I looked like a kid on a playground sticking her tongue out which is not the right way to do it. The mouth is closed, and the front of the tongue is just resting. You'll know you've got it right when your breath naturally flows to fill the belly rather than expanding your chest. I practice this breath when I am anxious, feel anger, need an energy boost, or want to reset my juju. I do it before I go in front of an audience to calm my body and my nerves.

It's also a good habit to get into when someone says something that annoys or offends you, and you need to collect your thoughts before responding. Shifting to a deeper breath will calm the stress in your body and give you a chance to regroup. I suspect this breathing technique would have helped me that day of the nerve block. As it was I did rely on breathing, but I instinctively used more of a labor-type breath with strong, long exhales through pursed lips. That breath winds you up for a fight, whereas this belly-breath, curled-tongue technique unwinds the tension. Different approaches for different circumstances.

The Ayurvedic doctor recommends learning to breathe with the back of the tongue dropped all the time. I haven't had the self-awareness to achieve this feat yet, although I can see the benefits of doing so should I ever set my mind to it.

The body is so incredibly powerful. It can heal itself and adapt to new circumstances and injuries. It can ignore pain when it needs to. It will provide adrenaline to get through intense times. It will even allow the female body to give birth and then willingly choose to go through the incredible pain more than once.

We can't underestimate the body's ability to overcome, and how it can be your greatest ally in your hardest times. But just because the body *can* push through doesn't mean it's healthy to constantly push it beyond its limits. There is a balance between compelling yourself to power through, and the need to rest and recharge. When you find the best way to honor your body's rhythms you will find your personal power.

I found that the more intentional I am about getting proper rest, the faster I get back to my best state. It works the other way too. Working in shorter, more focused stints, allows me to get back to rest faster. When I stay busy-busy and don't take the time to acknowledge the hurt and the emotional weights in my heart, recovery takes longer. It's the same when I exert a lot of intense energy, for example when I speak at a conference or do a training day for clients and then need to take it easy for a couple of days. My body does an equal swing on the pendulum. It goes "on," and then I need to allow it to turn "off." The longer I stay "on," the longer the crash will be on the other end.

Not all rest activities are created equally. Figure out the best way for your body to recover and rejuvenate. Some activities may seem helpful in the moment and yet they may be harmful in the long haul. Sitting static, while numbing out to TV or playing video games may feel good in the moment and offers some benefits when done within reason, but eventually these sedentary distractions cause other issues, such as boredom and an unfit body.

Sleep is the foundation of health. A proper night's slumber will recharge the body, but as discussed earlier, only when it is restful, nourishing sleep that allows you to heal. Figuring out how to get your Z's is important. Night after night people announce that they sleep awfully. Shockingly, this mantra, is at the front of their mind as they stare at the ceiling. Don't forget, the brain will deliver what you ask of it.

Arianna Huffington, founder of Thrive Global and the author of *The Sleep Revolution* was the impetus for me doing whatever it took to get a better sleep. I remember her sharing with an audience that even though she has four phones (at least she did at the time) she puts all electronics outside of her bedroom when she sleeps. Just this trick alone makes for a sounder slumber.

When I'm restless, Winston snuggles with me and I fall asleep much faster. Having him in my arms means I need to turn off the iPad (he doesn't like the light so he doesn't snuggle as much when it's on). I suspect that helps me fall asleep faster too. In addition to turning off technologies, or even moving them to another room, vitamins, relaxing bed time routines and quieting the looping messages in the brain by writing down problems can all make for a better sleep routine.

A relaxing hobby that allows you to get lost in enjoyment is a wonderful way to recharge. I think I'm most in my zone when I'm writing, which is usually more work than hobby and yet, doing so makes me feel peaceful. Hours can pass and suddenly I'll look up and realize how long I've been writing.

Sports can be rejuvenating, even if they're high-intensity. Many people say exercising helps them unwind, and it's certainly more beneficial to the body's health than watching Netflix. Any activity you enjoy, especially if it takes you outdoors for some fresh air and sunshine, can be positive. A walk, a workout, a swim, an exercise class, a trip to the spa; whatever it takes to care for your body is what you need to do – consistently.

Getting a massage once doesn't mean your muscles are free of stress forever. You need to keep feeding your body treats of love to keep it in optimal condition.

Make a list of what recharging exercises work for you, and rotate the options routinely.

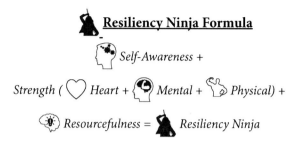

Resiliency Ninja Formula

Self-Awareness +

Strength (♡ Heart + Mental + Physical) +

Resourcefulness = Resiliency Ninja

 What techniques can you use to drown out your pain and hurts when you need to?

 Practice the back-of-the-tongue-smile breath to calm the body and direct oxygen deeper into your lungs.

 What activities are the most restful and rejuvenating for you? Make a list and rotate activities.

 Find your favorite places for body care and book regular appointments in advance for services such as massages, spa services, grooming and chiropractor treatments.

42

The Case of the Identity Snatchers

THE SURE-FIRE WAY TO LOSE your power is to let your adversity become your identity. Break-ups, chronic pain, business failures or any other adversity: if you're not careful, can consume you. In fact, adversity's very job is to test you and its goal is to take over your life. Don't let it.

I was at a party to celebrate the launch of a friend's business. It was enjoyable except that 10 minutes after my arrival my pain spiked sharply. I was talking with a contact about her business and suddenly the pain was like a lightning strike. "Bam, hello, take that, and that, and that again." Even though I was going through a severe pain attack, I did not let it interrupt the conversation. Without missing a beat, I kept listening intently.

It reminds me of when I was a little kid pulling on my dad's pant leg to get his attention while he was on the phone. No matter how annoying I was, he wouldn't skip a beat in his conversation.

That's how I perceive my pain, like a six-year-old begging for ice cream while Dad's on the phone. He knew I was there, and yet he wouldn't acknowledge my non-emergency until the appropriate time. (That's how it worked in the 1980s. I know now the protocol seems to be to interrupt the adult conversation to serve the child. Regardless, I hope the analogy still makes sense.)

Just because there's a knife stabbing into my body (or a child tugging for ice cream) doesn't mean I care any less about the person in front of me. There is nothing to be gained from bringing up the pain or complaining about it. All that would do is lose the momentum of an important conversation.

After the pain struck me at my friend's launch party, I excused myself when our conversation came to a natural pause. I went to the restroom and acknowledged my physical state to myself. Then mentally I blew up the hellish feeling, by focusing intensely on the source of the pain, calming my brain by reminding it that it's just nerves firing over actively, visualizing the cluster like it's a severe lightning storm, and just like a storm passes, I made peace with bolts of pain and asked them to dissipate so I could go back to mingling. It works until the lightning strikes again, and then I go through the process another time.

You and your adversity can co-exist harmoniously. It doesn't have to be a "you-against-it, life-or-death-round-robin-battle" every day.

You are not your pain. You have pain (or whatever your adversity is). Don't let it beat you. If debt is getting you down, don't see yourself as a financial failure; you're just a person who has a financial problem. Simple shift in semantics: major shift in implication.

Think of adversity as an undesired Grumpy Smurf with hands and feet and magical capabilities. Once this tiny blue gnome finds you and attaches to your brain, it duct-tapes itself onto your life. There is no escaping Grumpy Smurf; he is with you for good. Every time you deny him and try to wish him away, he calls another Smurf to come for a visit. Now you have two Smurfs taped to your body, and two are harder to accept than one. If you focus all your energy on the two Smurfs, they'll say "Hey, this is great, look at all the attention we get attached to this person. Let's call some more friends." Next thing you know there are three of them, then four, and eventually you'll be covered in miniature, magical Smurfs pity-partying all over your body. You are no longer you because you've become a Smurf carrier. They have taken over your identity. People will see you and think, oh, there's that Smurf carrier.

The beauty is, you are still underneath all those Smurfs who are trying to suffocate you. If you make peace with the original Grumpy Smurf, he'll tell all his buddies to go away. The two of you will learn to co-exist in harmony and work together to help you achieve your dreams. Grumpy is now your partner in life.

The more you co-exist harmoniously, the less chance anyone will notice Grumpy tagging along. Maybe one day a miracle will occur and he'll get bored of you, and he'll disappear forever. But that's out of your control. Focus on controlling what you can.

There are many people who are covered with Smurfs, bent under the combined weight of their adversities. Yet there are also many people who walk around in a lively manner, with just one pain Smurf on their shoulder. It's up to you to decide how much you will let your adversity consume you.

It's easier to power through with one Smurf hanging around your body versus hundreds. For people who can't or won't control their Smurfs, it's hard to tell where their adversity ends and their identity begins. Instead of letting life's challenges engulf you, make peace with them by accepting the difficult emotions that come with your situation. Identify the obstacles or stresses they cause. Then focus on creating techniques for working around the issues that are within your control. That's how you keep adversity from taking over your life.

You need trusted friends who have your back to tell you when the Smurfs have snatched your identity. It's usually the people closest to us who can see when things aren't quite right. Mom plays this role and is a good reminder when I'm letting my pain take over.

My earlier story of feeling pain at the party and not skipping a beat is just one way to manage your social experiences. Contrast that with another pain patient I know. She has let pain rule her life and her professional image. She walks around business events using a pain hobble, wearing a pain face telling everyone who will listen about her pain story. There is no doubt she is in pain, I get it. We all get it, and we know it's tough.

But she acts as if she wants everyone to sympathize with her by feeling her same pain. It doesn't work that way. The energy around her is so destructive that people just don't respond to her the way they did before she was consumed by her pain. Back then she did her hair and brushed her teeth and took pride in her appearance. Not anymore. She is one big miniature, magical Smurf carrier, and people avoid her because of it.

That's the power adversity can have on people. If you want to show up as your very best, you can't let the pain of life win. Tough times need to be honored, no doubt, but they can't rule your life, and they mustn't trickle into your professional realm. I've met people who are in wheelchairs or suffering from fibromyalgia who have smiles on their faces and authentically see the joy around them, even with those difficult hardships. They are inspiring. They have conversations that don't revolve around their physical limitations and they take interest in other people and their pursuits.

What's the difference between the smiling people and the miserable pain patients? Do the people who spread joy feel less pain? I doubt it. People's hurts are based on their perception, and no doubt they perceive their circumstances as just as dire as mine or yours. What makes the difference is the story they tell around the pain, and how willing they are to allow the tough times to consume other aspects of their life.

Rarely do people see my pain or hear about it, because I've shrunk my Smurf so much that I can control my reaction even when it gets especially grumpy. The early days, though, were very tough going, and while I would collapse at home I still tried to keep a convincing face out in public. If I would have understood this perspective and the brain's power to influence pain, I would have made fewer mistakes throughout the early years.

Shrink your Smurfs. Make friends with them and put them in your pocket so you can focus on the task at hand – achieving success and fulfillment no matter what gets thrown at you.

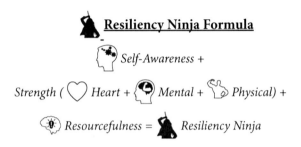

Resiliency Ninja Formula

Self-Awareness +

Strength (Heart + Mental + Physical) +

Resourcefulness = Resiliency Ninja

  Have you let your adversities consume your identity?

  Are you letting your grooming falter because of your adversities, obstacles and stressors?

Acknowledge your adversities for what they are and make peace with their existence so you can co-exist in harmony.

43

The Power of a Poker Face

I HAVE ABSOLUTELY NO GAME face when playing poker. In fact, on the few occasions I've played in charity poker tournaments, I purposely take money for a couple extra rounds of buy-in because I am notorious for losing so quickly. Poker is not my forte.

But when it comes to putting on a brave face in public I'm a master. In the early days, I felt I had no choice. I had a certain reputation to maintain. The year before the surgery I had over-filled my days and nights so I had set the bar high.

A few years after the original surgery, I was still trying to maintain a calm outward appearance. I had long been known for bringing people together and being a master at networking. That topic launched my company, so it made sense that I would continue to host networking events.

A friend and I decided to host a cocktail party for 70 of our closest business associates in the party room of my building. It was a huge success. People were mingling and friends were cross-connecting, which I love to see. As the night wore on, however, I could feel my adrenaline and excitement fade while my pain surged. What was I to do? Many of the people there had no idea about my surgeries. My role was to play the hostess with the mostest. There was no way I was putting on a pain face and letting down my guests.

The moment the last guest walked out the door I literally collapsed onto the pool table, and eventually to the floor. Four of my closest friends were in the room, and they already knew the story. They hung with me until I was physically able to walk to the elevator, get upstairs, and crawl into bed. This was a classic example of losing at Whack-a-Mole. I was smiling on the outside and experiencing excruciating pain on the inside.

When my pain was extra bad it didn't matter how much of a smile I tried to plaster on my face, the people who knew me the best could tell something wasn't right. The night of the cocktail party, one of my best friends kept checking in to ask how I was doing. She could see the desperation behind my eyes and saw it getting progressively worse throughout the night. I didn't have to tell her, she just knew and was willing to sit on the floor with me after the party for as long as it took.

Strangers or new contacts wouldn't have known anything was wrong. They were oblivious, and that's a good thing.

My double standard of wanting to be authentic in the moment while keeping a deep, difficult secret is the "great internal divide" in action. Just because you're going through a difficult time doesn't mean everyone has the right to hear the story. Honing your poker face allows you to choose what you want to reveal and to whom you wish to reveal it.

When faced with adversity, there are times when you want to shine as if there is absolutely nothing wrong – for instance, when you're in front of clients or new prospects. And there are times when you have to let go of the charade and shed tears in a safe place, with people you trust.

Mind you, there were many days when I wasn't quite as strong with my fake-it so you can make-it image. Usually if I know I can't wear a poker face I won't go to an event, or I'll bail early. Sometimes despite my best intentions my lack of "ON-ness" catches me off guard.

The summer before I started writing this book, I was at a charity Dragon Boat Race. Everyone was having fun, playing cards, visiting and enjoying some snacks on the lawn before we had to race again and I, Miss-Always-Have-To-Be-ON, fell asleep right there on the grass while the rest of the team was mingling around me. Of course, I was embarrassed, but the people who knew understood there was physically nothing I could do but nap when I had to.

So where do you draw the line? When do you put on airs and act like nothing is wrong and when do you say the honest truth – that you're going through hell and if they don't mind you'd like to sob uncontrollably on their shoulder or at least have the option to be OFF?

Well, I'm of the opinion that being phoney never works in the long run, which may sound counterintuitive to the point of this chapter. You'll need to find a balance that feels authentic for you.

Unless someone else can learn from your struggle, be entertained by it or leverage it for their own gain, aside from very close family and friends, no one really cares about your problems. That means that in front of clients, prospects, professional contacts and associates who aren't in your inner circle, the poker face may be your best bet.

The perfect poker face is not really about pretending everything is great when you're in the middle of a shit storm, it's more about showing the best side of you and not revealing your other cards. The trouble is people can sense when something is not aligned even if they can't put their finger on it. That sensation that something isn't quite right can make it difficult for people to trust you. Plus, it widens your great internal divide, because not only do you think you need to be able to be better than your authentic self is in that moment, now you are forcing yourself to act in a way that isn't aligned and doesn't feel good.

Therefore, to remain authentic and stay positive, even when you don't feel positive, the key is to find something – anything – that is going really well. As I mentioned earlier, there are always blessings that balance our difficulties; it's up to you to be clear on what your blessings are. If you have to struggle to think of your blessings, then make a list and carry it with you everywhere you go as a reminder.

In this book, I hope you have learned to arm yourself by beefing up your internal focus on the aspects of your life that give you the most joy. So, when someone asks how you are, instead of giving an inauthentic, overarching "Fantastic," which is a lie, or coming clean and saying, "Absolutely miserable," which is unprofessional, you can direct the conversation to something that is positive. It's the perfect place in-between misleading and oversharing.

For example, when someone asks you how work is going, you might tell a story about one client, a project you're diving into, or a new direction you're envisioning for the future. "Thanks for asking. I just booked a long weekend off and plan to go visit some family next weekend." or "Thanks for asking. Just last week I finally launched my new website, which is a huge weight off my shoulders." Or "Thanks for asking. I am expanding into the Chicago market and I'm really excited about the potential."

By being more specific about something positive that is happening professionally, you can maintain a conversation while deflecting attention away from your invisible game of Whack-a-Mole. Of course, this technique of offering an insightful answer to standard questions like, "How are you?" or "What's going on?" is a good conversation tactic even if you don't need an excuse to avoid sharing a hidden secret. Specific, personal answers to broad questions create more interesting chit-chat. It forces the topic to go deeper than typical superficial banter.

When you answer the question "How's work?" with a simple "great," there is no launching pad to make for an interesting conversation. When you respond enthusiastically by mentioning a project you're passionate about, the other person's interest will be piqued.

Now, I have to admit that before I figured out these strategies, I had some bad days when I just couldn't maintain a poker face. The failed lunch story I shared in the first chapter is a good example. It was as if I had all my chips in the pot, and everyone at the table could see my cards were a mishmash of nothingness.

So yes, you need a poker face to get by during tough times, but you don't have to bluff, just be smooth enough to keep the pot in play. Focus on what is positive and true, and build your small talk around those small wins, however unimportant they may seem amidst the big picture. If you miss a few hands because you just can't keep it together, no worries. Buy in again and play smarter with your new knowledge.

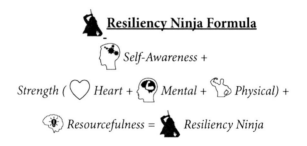

Resiliency Ninja Formula

Self-Awareness +

Strength (♡ Heart + Mental + Physical) +

Resourcefulness = Resiliency Ninja

   Who are the people in your circle of trust with whom you can share your full truth, and who needs to see a more distanced view?

   Direct your conversations in positive directions that are authentic and honest, rather than oversharing details about what's going wrong in your life.

   Do you have a good poker face? What can you do to bring your A-game when it counts, even when your world is falling apart around you?

44

Then There Is the Pain Face

REMEMBER WHEN YOU WERE A kid and didn't want to go to school? You'd put on the, "Oh, I'm so sick, puppy-dog eyes" pain face for your parents. Did you ever see that pain face in the mirror? It isn't pretty. It's like catching a glimpse of yourself crying and turning those tears into laughter because the image is so uncharacteristic of your natural state.

The difference between looking like you're in pain and looking like a superstar, is written on your face and in how you carry yourself.

If you and I were in a room together, regardless of my current pain level, I could put on either a pain face or a happy face. I could make the happy face genuine by focusing on the blessings in my life that inspire happiness, despite the adversities swarming around me. The story you tell the outside world is completely within your control.

Most of the time in public, when you look at me you would never think I'm in pain. Why? It's because I choose not to wear my pain face. Even at the hospital post surgeries I'm still conscious of how a smile will brighten both my state and the state of others around me. No one is attracted to a pouty-pain-face.

The state of your face will influence how you feel too. Nine times out of 10, wearing a pain face makes you feel more pain, whereas a smiley face inspires increased happiness that blocks out some of the pain.

I remember one resident doctor saying to me, dubiously, "Well, you don't look like you're in that much pain."

"Oh, really? How do you want me to look? Like a victim? Why do I have to wear a pouty pain face for you to understand the severity of what it's like to live in my body? I just won't do it." That doesn't mean I didn't have breakdowns in doctors' offices, I did. I just wasn't going to walk around looking like a pain patient 24/7. Doing so, would not be of service to anyone, especially me.

One of the greatest factors in resiliency is controlling how dramatic the story is around your problems, and by positively influencing the story with your body language, you can inspire momentum in the right direction.

Some people who have pain or feel stressed, don't *want* to change their pain face. They want to validate their pain by having others understand just how hard they have it, or even better, join them in the depths of their misery. There's no doubt, misery loves company, and by signaling others with a pain face, those with compassion will have to ask, "What's wrong?"; thereby giving the person with the pain the chance to bring others into their negative vortex and provoke empathy.

The goal is not to delete a bad emotion or deny a difficult circumstance by eliminating the pain face. You're simply trying to come at any problem from the most optimistic angle possible. You can't do that when you're being Mr. Pouty Pouterton.

Your face is trying to align with your internal emotions, whether that means your insides becoming happier to match your smile, or your insides wallowing in self-pity to match your pout. It's up to you to decide which direction your heart will be led. Smiles attract smiles, internally and externally. Period.

I love walking through an airport making eye contact with people and shooting them huge smiles. People respond with an extra pep in their step.

Practice turning off your pain-face or your stress-face, or any other facial emotion that doesn't serve you or the people seeing it. I dare you to smile a HUGE smile or try one of the other positive state-changing ideas mentioned in this book, the next time you feel down. Let me know how it worked for you. Doesn't it make you feel better? When you're controlling your face and mood, you can approach any obstacles with a more optimistic viewpoint; like a Resiliency Ninja.

Resiliency Ninja Formula

Self-Awareness +

Strength (Heart + Mental + Physical) +

Resourcefulness = Resiliency Ninja

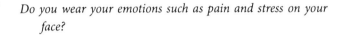

Do you wear your emotions such as pain and stress on your face?

How good are you at making a pain face? When was the last time you looked in the mirror when you saw it? It's completely out of character, right?

Change your face, change your state.

Your heart will move to reflect the expression on your face.

45

Loop-dee-loo

As you may imagine, there were times through all of this adversity where I couldn't find a poker face, or even a pain face. You might call it the stoned-but-didn't-realize-it face. While nowadays I don't take medication to control my pain, it took years of exploring chemical concoctions before I found a pain medication that relieved my nerve pain and didn't cause major side effects. Before that there were days when I had no idea how much the medication affected me. I would be so stoned, I didn't even realize how my brain was altered. It wasn't just the medication, either. When you're going through grief, the overwhelming numbing sensation can have the same impact as some of the worst narcotics.

Thankfully, I did not ever form a dependency on medications. The doctors made it clear that the key to avoiding an addiction to pills is to only take exactly what you need to cover the pain, and never take more. It's when you take pills beyond your pain threshold that your body craves them. My body was the opposite. Some medications caused a violent reaction, even with a small dose, whereas others were subtle, building slowly and then shifting my personality. Mom was quick to notice the changes, and I would get back to the doctors quickly to stop taking the meds once I realized their adverse reaction.

Before I found the medication that worked, I was in excruciating pain. I had tried a new medication that just wasn't jiving well at all, but it took me a while to recognize that. I had a meeting with the new director of a training program that happened to be my largest client. They were my baseline bread and butter for the early years of my decade of hell.

It was a Monday morning in Toronto. I dressed in a power suit and was ready to wow the new decision maker. How hard could this be, I thought?

Unfortunately, I was reacting to the new pain meds and it wasn't pretty. My eyes were glazed over, I was slurring my words and the pain was intense. I slouched in the chair trying to get comfortable – like a drunken party-goer at the end of a long night. I can't say for certain that I didn't drool or make inappropriate comments, but there is a high probability I did all of that and worse.

Despite my minimal recollection, I am confident that the meeting went terribly wrong because she didn't like me one bit. Even though I was the top-rated presenter for their program for years running, I lost the gig. She was probably trying to figure out who was this loop-dee-loo lady everyone thinks is so great at training people on how to build business relationships. I tried several times to reconnect once I was off those meds, but apparently, her good opinion once lost was lost forever.

That was an expensive mistake.

Why do I share this embarrassing story? Well, for two reasons.

First, so you can see that sometimes it's just better to cancel and take care of your body. Cancelling the meeting, although hardly ideal, would have done less damage than showing up in an unprofessional way.

Second, because it's important to know that no matter how resilient you think you are, there are times when you just can't manage that superhero pose. It's more like curling up in a ball of a blubbering mess.

Even a Resiliency Ninja loses a battle every now and again.

Resiliency Ninja Formula

Self-Awareness +

Strength (Heart + Mental + Physical) +

Resourcefulness = Resiliency Ninja

 When your body is not cooperating, cancelling gracefully is better than blowing your chance to make the right first impression.

 Advocate for your own health. If you take medications, notice the side effects and don't be shy about going back to your health care professional to get it checked.

46

The Bliss List

KIM, A FRIEND FROM HIGH SCHOOL, has gone on to become a family therapist. It's not surprising given she was always excellent at giving advice, even when we were teenagers.

This past summer she came for a visit. We hadn't seen each other in years. During our patio time, we talked about destructive recurring patterns and how to rewrite your expectations for life. She is committed to helping people shift their attitudes to find peace and joy amidst the mundane responsibilities of life.

One exercise Kim shared is called the Bliss List that she hangs on her fridge.

When you're in a good mood, preferably before adversity overshadows your vision, write a list of 20 or more low-cost, low-hassle activities that you enjoy. For example, a picnic in the park, a hike through the woods, a swim in the community pool, a visit to the local bird sanctuary, or playing hide-and-seek with your kids. It doesn't matter what's on the list, just so long as they are things that make you feel happy. Every time you are feeling sad, change your state by looking at the list and choosing one of the activities to do immediately. If you do something that you know will bring you joy, then you can snap out of your negative rut.

This is such a useful tool, and so easy to implement.

I find that when I'm in a rut, the first activities that go are usually the healthiest, such as exercise. Without a workaround that motivates me to get some exercise, days can easily pass before I get out and do some activity. I knew that the right kind of exercise on a regular basis would make me feel better, so I set out to find a way to consistently make it a priority without getting bored.

Ultimately, I created the Resiliency Ninja Healthy Living Cards. You can order your own custom set at www.R-Ninja.com. They changed the exercise game for me.

What I did was write down several different exercises I enjoy that wouldn't aggravate my pain. My list included swimming, hot yoga and walking in the park with Winston. Then I created a positive challenge to associate with each activity. For example, swim for 30 minutes, paying attention to your stroke, or 30 minutes of swimming focusing on your breathing technique. Each of these challenge activities, mixed with a motivational message, became a card.

Then each morning (you can use them weekly to plan ahead) I pulled one card from the pile to ensure I completed at least one activity that day. If I pulled a card that I didn't feel like doing or the task didn't suit my energy level, I pulled a second card and did that one instead. Often I'd feel better after that activity and challenged myself to do both. Eventually I started wishing I was pulling the swimming card every day, so I just use the cards when I feel like a change in activity or notice I'm not exercising enough. The cards have been effective in motivating me to exercise in a way that includes a lot of variety.

Another mood-changing tool is positive self-help books and videos. Reading, watching or listening to my favorite business experts and influencers is not just relaxing, but gives me new energy and motivation.

Podcasts are an easy and free option to getting great motivational content. Please be sure to check out the Resiliency Ninja podcast. Each week, I interview guests to uncover stories of stress, obstacles and adversity behind the success story and offer insights in the FU-CHAAA Friday episodes. www.R-Ninja.com/podcast to listen for free!

To enhance your darkest days, find things to do that will help you see the silver lining. A friend gave me a Little Blue Book of Inspiration when I was going through some tough times. It was a nice pick-me-up to access in difficult moments. There are lots of other books I'll grab when I feel down. Of course, journaling is one of the most powerful things you can do to find your bliss.

Whatever approaches you choose, always keep a list of positive activities, reminders and confidence-boosters close to you. This will give you a way to snap out of feeling sorry for yourself when things get tough. When we're feeling sad or faced with adversity, it's usually hard to think of happiness-inducing activities. These lists are a great tool for anticipating bleak times and for reminding you that even though one aspect of your life may be going off the rails, there are wonderful things happening in your life as well.

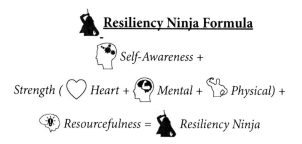

Resiliency Ninja Formula

Self-Awareness +

Strength (♡ *Heart +* 🧠 *Mental +* 🏃 *Physical) +*

🐑 *Resourcefulness =* 🥷 *Resiliency Ninja*

 Create a Bliss List and post it on your fridge. When you're feeling blue, go to the list and choose from one of the 20 low-cost, easy-to-do-on-a-whim activities to turn around your mood.

 Order your custom Resiliency Ninja Healthy Living Cards at www.R-Ninja.com

 Subscribe to my Resiliency Ninja podcast for Free on your favorite podcast platform. www.R-Ninja.com/podcast

 Keep a book of inspiration or a collection of motivational quotes handy to help you see the silver lining in tough times.

 Reach for a journal and write a series of empowering and clarifying statements to identify positive statements to overshadow negative limitations.
For example:
- My ….. is hurting but I can still ….
- I cannot …, but I can…

47

F@#&. This Hurts. Let's Get to It

For years, every morning I woke up and my first thought was "F@#&, this hurts." My second thought was, "What needs to get done today to keep my business alive?" My goal was to complete the three most important tasks required and if I managed to do anything else on the day's to-do circle, it was a bonus. My baseline nerve pain, plus all the other adversities thrown my way, forced me to get really good at identifying my top priorities and the level of focus inspired me to power through to get them done, no matter what my body or heart were saying.

An organization that has been really valuable on my journey is the Canadian Association of Professional Speakers (CAPS), which is affiliated with the National Speakers Association (NSA) in the U.S., and with the Global Speakers Federation (GSF).

At one speakers' conference, I talked with a veteran member who had been named to the Speakers' Hall of Fame. At the time my business was doing well, but I had this dark cloud hanging over my head as I wondered if my physical or emotional pain would stop me from speaking at a client event. Would I ever have to cancel because I was too sore?

I asked him, have you ever been sick and had to cancel an event? "Never," he said. "I don't care how sick I am or what's going on in my life. I can pull myself together to do anything for an hour."

This was a pivotal confidence builder for me. He was right; I had felt the stimulating effects of adrenaline when I was on stage, too. I knew that no matter how much I wanted to collapse before getting on stage, once I was up on the stage I would block out all the pain and focus solely on serving my audience.

After my first nose surgery to reset the break from the tire that hit my face, I woke up from the surgery and my first thought was, "F@#&. This hurts." The next thing I did was ask the doctor, "When can I go?" Confused, he asked, "Go where?" What I didn't tell the doctor before surgery was that I had a client workshop booked for the next day and I had no intention of cancelling.

It turns out that the protocol for recovering from surgery does not include driving two hours to present a four-hour workshop the next morning. The docs and nurses were adamant I wouldn't be able to do it. They thought I was crazy. They didn't understand that I didn't have the luxury to sit and heal until I completed my client gig. For now, I was in solution-finding mode.

My mom had recently undergone knee-replacement surgery, so she wasn't able to drive yet, but she needed to stay with me overnight because after anesthetic a patient shouldn't be left alone for 24 hours. Fortunately, one of my CAPS colleagues was available to be our chauffeur. On a moment's notice, he came to the hospital, picked Mom and me up and drove us to Toronto to drop us at our hotel. Talk about the CAPS spirit being alive and well! Along the way we stopped to buy white medical tape from the pharmacy to cover the blood that had seeped onto my nose cast. (In hindsight, a dab of White-Out might have worked better.)

The next morning, I showed up for my client with a smile on my face (as best as I could muster, given the nose cast and continuing pain), and got to work. For the entire morning, my nose did not drip a drop of blood and I blocked out the pain by focusing solely on delivering value for my client.

The second I got back to my hotel room after the workshop, blood started gushing out of my nose. It didn't stop for days.

Why the blood didn't flow in front of the audience, I don't know. Was it adrenaline, luck, God's blessing or angels stuffing invisible tissue in my nose? Whatever the good graces are that got me through that day, I am just thankful.

The follow-up nose reconstruction surgery was a different story. I was black and blue and swollen, and almost unrecognizable. I now understand that this is a typical outcome of nose surgery. (It's another blessing that my face did not react to the first surgery that way.) Since the second procedure was planned, thankfully, I was able to schedule lots of recovery time.

Sometimes we don't give our body enough credit that it will get us through when we absolutely, positively have to deliver. Instead of cancelling a commitment as a first response to trauma, why not see if you can power through it instead? You may surprise yourself. Just be sure to book the necessary downtime after you've delivered the goods, because powering through is a technique to be used in a pinch, not as a way of life.

What boundaries will you set for yourself? Will your default position be to cancel, or are there times when you will choose to power through?

Every time I am forced to dig deep and find courage to do something despite the pain or grief or disbelief in myself, I'm reminded of the advice I got from my CAPS colleague and I say, "I can do anything for an hour. I know it hurts, but let's do this."

Resiliency Ninja Formula

Self-Awareness +

Strength (♡ Heart + Mental + Physical) +

Resourcefulness = Resiliency Ninja

Are you using your physical or emotional pain as excuses not to succeed? What would it take to push yourself just a bit further than the voice of defeat thinks you should?

Your body can endure difficult situations. Give it a chance to show you its strength.

Be grateful every time you are blessed to power through a commitment and honor yourself when you truly just can't and have to focus on healing instead.

Do you have a group of people or an association that has your back, and will help you through tough times? If not, find one.

48

Days that Vanish

MANY DAYS VANISHED MYSTERIOUSLY BEFORE I could get all my tasks done. You may have noticed this too.

As the punches were coming at me, I found that my work productivity was still high. But as the perceived punches grew fewer in number, my productivity went down. It seemed counterintuitive.

The reason is because in the thick of things, I honored time like the precious resource it is.

It's simple to consume days with unimportant tasks and let other people's expectations overshadow your own priorities.

Very often the projects that meant the most to me like writing articles, making sales calls or spending quality time with family and friends, would get pushed to "tomorrow" once again.

One day I was so frustrated. I hadn't made any of the sales calls I needed to make. At 5:15PM I wrote down everything I did that day. There were 16 items on the list. Not bad I thought; maybe I am doing more than I think I am. As I went through the items, I calculated that eight could have been done by someone else, five items I shouldn't have done at all, and only three were classified as important.

I encourage you to take a similar inventory of everything you do in a day – or even better, a whole week. Chances are you complete a lot of tasks on autopilot, so they're not being done in the most effective way. By noting those inefficiencies, you can create more productive systems.

Simply carry a note pad or a calendar with pre-printed time slots. Every time you do a task, jot it down and note roughly how long it took. By doing this continuously, in real time, you can also note the time of day you did the task and, if you're really serious, capture a comment about your energy level in the moment. Real-time tracking is better than recapping at the end of the day, because you can just glance at a clock and record your current emotion. That data will come in handy with these productivity ideas I'm going to share.

Review your list and divide your task into four categories: the most important, the busy work, the stuff that could be delegated and those that could be deleted. The day after I reviewed my list of 16 accomplishments I hired an assistant for $20 an hour to work for a few hours a week. It was a minor investment in buying back precious hours of my time.

A major influencer of your productivity is your body's rhythm. There are times you'll feel productive and times when you'll feel depleted. These ebbs and flows are generally quite predictable. Finding your cadence allows you to tap into your best times for being productive. Then you can expect yourself to thrive when you're in your highs, and produce less when you're in a dip.

To get you started, here's a glimpse of my calendar, and my highs and lows.

My most productive focus time is first thing in the morning. If I dabble in unproductive or unimportant things to start my day, it is even harder to shift gears later into full-focus mode. Despite trying to emulate some of the great business minds who have elaborate morning routines including a work out, meditation and journal writing, despite recognizing the importance of these activities, I finally accepted that a busy personal-development morning routine doesn't work for my body. I can do those types of activities after the workday is complete. I find setting my intention for the day the night before, and with a few minutes of gratitude as I wake, is more impactful than doing the full mindset and body priming routine first thing.

In the afternoon, my pain usually spikes – even now – so I plan to lie down or at least take a break. I'm an excellent napper. I can pull off a full REM cycle and then start the second half of my day feeling alert and refreshed.

Another rhythm is that after intense activity such as speaking for an audience, I need time to recover physically. I block time for rest rather than expecting myself to run from one event to another. When I travel for a keynote I lay low the day before I go and plan lower-intensity days after I get home. I rarely go for a late dinner or socialize the night before I speak at a conference.

Recognizing your body's best and worst times for productivity helps you schedule accordingly. Don't book low-profitability activities in high productivity times. I protect my morning power-sessions and mid-afternoon refreshes like gold.

If I exercise it's later in the day, when my brain is spent. I take Winston to the park in the early evening. If you see me in the park mid-morning, it's either because I've been up since the wee hours of the morning and I've already accomplished my three priority tasks for the day, or because I've decided it's a recovery day.

When are you most productive? Are you doing your most important activities during that time, or are you wasting that time doing busy work?

To avoid having your work schedule disturbed, set boundaries with family or co-workers. Let them know you will connect with them after your high-focus hours are over. You'll get more done in less time using this method. That means you'll have more time to serve the other people's needs, without having work guilt hanging over your shoulders. They'll gladly leave you alone while your timer is ticking so they can experience focused time with you later. It's the constant half-engaged, half-working interactions that make the people close to you feel starved for attention.

Once you find your rhythm, the feeling of accomplishment that comes from focused results fuels the rest of your day.

There is a four-point daily priority plan on my whiteboard. It says Happy Clients, Lots of Sales, Thoughtful Marketing and Admin. The goal each day is to focus my activities on those four criteria and in that order. "Admin" is the busy work; it's often the least challenging. Checking emails, tinkering with contract templates or booking travel are examples of items that you should never do during your peak productivity hours.

I prioritize tasks that keep clients happy. Then I move to proactively reaching out to prospects. Then I dive into marketing that I believe will get me closer to my prime prospects. Only then, if I have energy left, will I do the busy admin stuff that comes with running a business. If you never get to the admin, no problem, by focusing on the other three priorities you can use the additional profits to hire an assistant or bookkeeper to look after the busy work for you.

Since I started this book six months before its publish date, several hundred hours have been focused on creating content and writing. I made a conscious decision to veer away from my daily priorities in order to accommodate this larger project. On the days when I didn't work on the book, I was super focused on the daily priorities and found the most efficient ways to get the necessary work done in the least amount of time.

Approaching daily tasks the same way you always have, either randomly or on virtual autopilot, sucks precious time. Guaranteed, there are better, more efficient and more productive ways of tackling those activities. Too often we find that we're spending too much time doing the tasks that don't matter or doing the tasks that do matter in the most inefficient way possible.

My focus on the most important tasks was inspired when I read the work of management expert Peter Drucker, one of the world's great authorities on getting things done. The influential insight I gained that increased my productivity didn't even come from his famous book, The Effective Executive; it was the add-on, leather-bound workbook that made the difference for me. I opened it to a page that asked the simple question, "What do you actually get paid to do?" Great question! Wow, did it change my perception of how I spent my days. My natural state is to waste time with a lot of activities that I may enjoy, but don't earn me money. While I'm blessed to have the freedom to lollygag, I feel more content when I focus more frequently on doing the best activities to drive my business.

I really felt I found an extra level of control over my self-management after watching a 2015 TEDx Douglasville talk by Rory Vaden called "How to Multiply Your Time." His theory on productivity offers a paradigm shift. He recommends you spend time on things today that will give you more time tomorrow. This is brilliant advice.

When you look at your tasks and learn how much time it takes you to do things, you may notice patterns that could eliminate a task altogether, or other work that could be automated with the right systems, which in return would free more time next week. The catch is, it takes time to implement new systems, and who has time to do that? So instead, you stay busy-busy, never getting the right things done and complaining that the days just vanish. Instead, sit down and look objectively at how you're spending your time. Take steps to get back every minute you can.

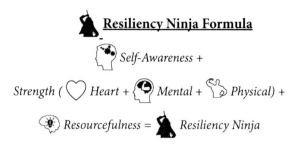

Resiliency Ninja Formula

Self-Awareness +

Strength (Heart + Mental + Physical) +

Resourcefulness = Resiliency Ninja

How are you spending your time?

What are your daily productivity patterns? Do you schedule the highest-importance activities in peak times, or in your lulls?

Track the tasks you do each day. Then determine if each task has high or low value, and which can be delegated or deleted.

Create systems today to buy time tomorrow.

Set a specific time to create mini-focus sessions. I like to turn off all distractions for 75 minutes at a time. Focused effort inspires greater results faster.

Create a Daily Priority Focus for each day. Mine is Happy Clients, Lots of Sales, Thoughtful Marketing, and then Admin.

Can you hire an assistant, get a volunteer, engage a co-op student, or swap services with someone to do your admin tasks for you, so you can focus on the important aspects of your role?

49

Controlling Your Schedule

YOUR NUMBER ONE PRIORITY IS to get really good at figuring out your priorities. What activities give you the most bang for your buck? Anything that won't contribute to making the greatest strides can move to the back burner as you focus on what's most important while you are healing from your adversities.

There were lots of times I let a lot of little things slide because I had to choose where to focus my limited resources. Did those little things matter in the grand scheme? Nope. Sure, maybe I would have gained more clients or additional media coverage by doing all those other little things, but to what end? I was already at capacity. My reality was that all I could produce was the bare minimum. By making sure those efforts focused only on high-priority items, I was able to earn a good living and make a positive impact on the world. Even if it didn't match my original expectations for myself, I still felt happy with what I could achieve in such a small amount of time.

Activities that required less intensity and focus like paying the bills, managing social media or returning emails to non-clients or non-prospects were often completed in non-peak energy times while I was stretched out in bed, on the couch or waiting in a doctors' office. Why waste prime sitting time doing something that wasn't going to help my livelihood? If the quality of a task wasn't gravely impacted by doing it when I was exhausted, then it could wait. By contrast, making sales calls in low-energy times would not be a smart idea.

Some days would be heavier than others, but a typical routine could have been, 1) write an article, 2) prep for a client event, 3) call a prospect. That was anywhere from two to three hours of work and I would be satisfied with my effort. After those activities were complete I could open my day to tasks of lesser importance. If I caught a second wind later in the afternoon after my siesta, then I would tackle another priority item until I ran out of steam.

Chunking my calendar was another strategy that transformed my productivity. Basically, you look at all the results you want to achieve and the actions that make them come to life. For example, your business may have four or five basic activities that need to happen every day. As a business owner, you may need to serve clients, sell, market and do all the other busy admin work that keeps a business alive. As an employee, you will have a list of actions that fit your job description.

Find the themes among the various items in your to-do circle. For example: errands, client service, sales calls, creative development, social media, house work, exercise, cooking, networking meetings, visiting friends and family time. Don't forget time for healing and self-care, which should always be priorities – or all your other activities will suffer.

If you have several tedious tasks that must be done, such as errands, booking travel, invoicing or opening the mail, and you don't have a team member to do it for you, group all those tasks together for efficiency. Book a few hours on a Friday afternoon or another low-energy time to do all of the tasks that are required, but not urgent.

To honor your energy rhythms, map your priorities and commitments for the week. The way I do this is to scribble all the tasks I want to get done. Then I go through and give each an importance rating of A, B, C or D. Then I estimate how long each priority or task will take, and start grouping like-tasks together. The A's that take under 5 minutes each get done immediately after I am done planning for the week. That gives me a sense of accomplishment to launch the week.

With these prioritized tasks in hand, I turn my attention to a weekly calendar that displays each day hour-by-hour. I like an old-fashioned paper option for this activity even though it works equally well on an electronic calendar.

I review all my commitments that I can't change, such as client-training sessions, sales meetings or media appearances, and mark those times on the calendar. For example, every Tuesday morning I participate in a radio show, so nothing else gets booked in that time slot unless it is extraordinarily important like speaking at a conference. Next, I'll block out travel and recovery times for those priority meetings. I add appointments for pain recovery, naps and workout classes as part of my weekly planning. Once all the non-moveable items are scheduled, then I block the next group of activities together that have the highest level of priority. Since I know that I write best in the morning when I awake I'll earmark a chunk of time to get some creative prose completed on days when I have nothing else scheduled for the morning. I tend to get carried away typing so if I have an appointment in the morning, I make sure to set an alarm to remind me to get out of my reclining chair.

Ultimately the entire week is spoken for, including plenty of time for emergencies, rest, recovery, family and friends. It's also important to leave enough wiggle room in the schedule to be on time and stress-free. Trying to put too much into a day causes chronic lateness and unnecessary stress.

Many clients have told me that they try to book time for themselves – but inevitably those hours get sacrificed to clients or family or other urgent issues. It's up to you to protect and honor your calendar choices. No one else can do that for you. Find an accountability buddy or hire a coach who can hold you true to your word. (Hey, maybe I'm the coach for you. Check out my website for options.)

We all teach other people every day how to treat us. If you allow yourself to waver on your own issues, they won't hesitate to poke holes in all your best-laid plans.

If you treat your healing time with the same level of urgency as you treat your work commitments or the kids' soccer games, you'll be well on your way to becoming a Resiliency Ninja.

Resiliency Ninja Formula

Self-Awareness +

Strength (Heart + Mental + Physical) +

Resourcefulness = Resiliency Ninja

 How are you currently managing your time? Are you prioritizing?

 Do you schedule "ME" time for yourself? Who tends to intrude most on that time? Why do they believe they can do that? Why do you let them?

 If a task stays in your to-do circle for longer than 4 weeks without getting done, decide if it can be delegated or deleted. If you're not making it a priority, then why let it clog up the system?

 Write everything you need to get done onto a piece of paper. Next, categorize each as an A, B, C or D priority and estimate how much time it will take to complete each task.

 Get a master weekly calendar (paper or electronic) and start blocking off chunks of time for various tasks. Start with unmovable commitments, add in your self-care activities then fill in the remaining tasks, in descending order of importance.

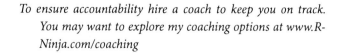 Find an assistant if that's feasible.

To ensure accountability hire a coach to keep you on track. You may want to explore my coaching options at www.R-Ninja.com/coaching

50

The Magic of Deadlines

WHEN I WROTE THE *People You Know* column, my deadline was 3:00 P.M. four days a week. If I started writing a column at 9:15 A.M., it was ready for 3:00. If I started to write at 2:15, it was ready for 3:00. The same was true when I wrote the *Getting Connected* column for the newspaper's business section, or when I wrote for any other publication. If I didn't have a deadline, as with the Huffington Post, I rarely got around to publishing there.

When faced with adversity, your mind can easily get swept up in daydreaming, and get lost in the challenges at hand. That changes when you go into survival mode and focus on getting a task done ahead of a tight deadline. The mind can only focus on one thing at a time, so if it's critical to send something to a client or complete a project for your boss, then your brain will make it happen.

This deadline inspiration has come in very handy when I'm having not-so-great days. I'll book a call with a client and promise to have something done before the call, giving me a hard deadline. This motivates me to pull out all the stops to deliver on time.

Artificially-manufactured deadlines are easily changed. It's really hard to trick yourself. Telling yourself you have to get this done by tonight, when your brain is saying, that's B.S. you really don't *have* to, doesn't work. That's why I always find a reason to make an artificial deadline a real deadline. It can be as simple as telling someone I'll have a product created by a certain day. My favorite is to borrow someone's cottage and commit to finish developing a product before I leave there. It keeps me focused on delivery. It's funny how generous people with cottages can be when you ask to borrow the quiet space specifically to finish a creative work.

If your network doesn't give you access to free retreats, find someplace quiet to completely focus on what you need to get done. It could be a bench in the park, a boardroom at a local shared space, or a quiet corner in a coffee shop. The key is to commit to not leaving until Project "X" is done. Don't do anything else. Phone and email notifications are off, headphones are on, and laptop is in hand with nothing active on-screen except the program you need to finish your project.

Focusing your effort means an assignment will take less time compared to when you dilly dally and "sort of" work on a project while trying to multitask. The less you allow your brain to drift when you're getting something done, the faster and more easily it will come to you. It will also make it possible to block out the hurt, frustration, grief, or whatever other emotions your adversity is stirring up.

Many people say they want to write a book, but they never get around to it because there's no critical deadline that pushes them to make it happen. Nice-to-haves almost always go out the window, but never more so than when adversity is knocking.

In 2008 I self-published my first book *Business Cards to Business Relationships: How to Build the Ultimate Network*. It took me 5 days to write (plus lots of editing after the fact) but that's because I had no choice. The political campaign was done, my money was gone and I needed something to give me an edge in the marketplace. If I hadn't prioritized a book to make money and open doors to clients, I would have never concentrated through the grueling process of writing a book in a hurry. I saw the book as the easiest way to position myself as a leading-edge speaker and make some money, so I had a real deadline. The sooner, the better.

That first book was my saving grace during the worst years of pain and grieving. I invested time up-front to make life better later. It allowed me to get on stages I wouldn't have been on otherwise, charge higher fees and serve audiences I wouldn't have dreamed of speaking for previously. It also opened doors to media appearances. In 2011 the publishing house John Wiley & Sons signed me, and within a year we had professionally published the second edition of my book called *From Business Cards to Business Relationships: Personal Branding and Profitable Networking Made Easy!* That edition took longer to produce because I didn't have the urgency driving me. (Check it out online at www.R-Ninja.com/books)

Whereas this book seems to be taking forever to write. Taking my own advice, I lit a fire on my timeline by declaring an official release date. Without that deadline, these words would not be flowing.

Resiliency Ninja Formula

Self-Awareness +

Strength (♡ Heart + Mental + Physical) +

Resourcefulness = Resiliency Ninja

 Do you work better with a looming deadline?

Deadlines are magic motivators that get your butt in gear. Use them to your advantage.

 Turn artificial deadlines into official ones by making a commitment to someone, preferably a person who expects you to stay true to your word, to complete the task by a certain time.

51

The Gloomy Cloud of Money Troubles

FINANCIAL TROUBLES CAN HANG OVER your head like a black cloud. They have the power to paralyze you and overshadow your enthusiasm for doing anything except worry.

If you are among the minority who spend less than you make and have never used a credit card or line of credit to stretch through a month, skip this chapter. You won't be able to relate with the rest of us.

This book would be incomplete if I didn't address the shame, embarrassment and emotional turmoil that money can have on the psyche. Next to grief and severe physical pain, I find that cash concerns rank among the most challenging of all obstacles.

The statistics around personal consumer debt are staggering, which leads me to believe that more people have debt than don't have it. So why is there such a huge stigma around it?

In some of the circles where I socialize, it's important to appear financially flush. People with less money may be envious of the appearance of those friends. They assume those people have it made with their fancy cars, exclusive club memberships and showy homes. But many of those rich-looking people are struggling, too – just on a bigger scale. Sure, there are the ultra-rich who have no clue what it's like to need overdraft protection, but that doesn't mean they will never feel a money crunch. If they overspend their fortune, they are screwed like the rest of us.

Many seemingly wealthy people have admitted to me that if they lost their source of income for more than a month or two, their entire lifestyle would blow up, and they would need to consider bankruptcy. The higher you ride, the further you have to fall.

There are many financial experts who are much better qualified than

I to guide you on the journey through the roller coaster ride of personal and business cash flow. If this is an issue for you then I urge you to find a personal finance guru or coach.

Having been on both sides – flush and broke – I've learned a lot over the years. Three lessons stand out for me.

First, it's a heck of a lot better to be on the "up" side of the money ride. The feeling of freedom and control that goes with being in the black is worth every sacrifice it takes to get and stay there. Even so, money does not absorb you from life's shocks. It is only one resource, and probably less valuable in the long run than talent, emotional intelligence, determination, your family and your network.

Second, money is fluid. It comes, it goes, it comes back again. The sooner you can detach emotionally from what's in your bank account, the sooner you'll feel in control of your finances.

Third, wishing for the lottery win or pie-in-the-sky deals will leave you frustrated. Constantly aiming for the big wins and dismissing the small wins along the way can add to your money troubles.

So many people are hoping for a magic wand that will take the weight of the world off their shoulders. If you could just win enough money to pay everything off, get back to zero and start fresh then life would be perfect – right? Counting on the lottery win leaves you completely vulnerable to the randomness of Powerball, and that's a recipe for being disappointed again and again, week after week. Even if you got the big win, it would not make your troubles disappear.

Most people who win the lottery go bankrupt because they squander their winnings. They haven't learned how to have discipline around money yet.

I've had the big wins. Not from the lottery, but from huge client contracts. You've heard the phrase, "The more you make, the more you spend." Your life will consume whatever money you leave for it. I'm not alone in this, it's the way most people are. No big win will erase bad financial habits. Only you can do that.

That's why it's imperative to take the money you want to save or use to pay off debt out of your main account immediately. You won't miss what you don't see. I realized that if I didn't reduce the amount of credit available to me, I could be tempted to rack it up to the limit. So as a card was paid off, I would eliminate that borrowing room by cutting up the card or closing the account. I did whatever it took to stop the cycle. When debt is used as a resource, it has the potential to creep back to the limit. So be aware of that reality and take steps to protect yourself from it.

The down swings in my finances made everything else more difficult. My stress was higher, my sleep was worse, and my pain increased. As anyone who has had money troubles before knows, it can be emotionally all-encompassing. Especially for an entrepreneur. You have no salary, and probably not much of a pension. You may not know where your next client is coming from. And you may have the pressures of payroll and other fixed costs that have to be met every month before you get a penny. Wow, can that be stressful.

First thing to do is to accept that fluidity of money is a part of life. Stop hating yourself if you've made a financial mess. While it may be your responsibility, I don't think that the inability to manage money is your fault. Most schools don't teach even a second of personal finance. So, most of us are at the mercy of our parents' money habits, which they would have picked up from their parents. It's the luck of the draw. Now, as an adult, it's up to you to decide if you're going to break the cycle if bad money habits are part of your family's culture.

Next, decide that you are going to proactively manage your emotions around money so you can focus on finding a solution instead of wallowing. When you're driving, if you stare at the telephone poll that you don't want to hit, guess what, you're going to hit it. It's the same thing with money. If you focus and worry for hours on end about your debt, guess what you're going to get more of? Debt. It's more advantageous to focus on how to get out of debt, rather than stress about the big number.

To get unstuck, take responsibility for where you are now. Create a system to monitor your finances without letting your worries spin out of control. Be aware of your debt, but don't obsess over it.

To keep me on track, my bookkeeper sends me a weekly report on everything I've spent and where I am financially, so I can keep tabs on my fiscal reality. Without that information, my imagination swirls and can magnify any issues that may be looming. In the old days, I didn't know exactly what I owed, but I knew it wasn't good.

Now that I know exactly where my money is, and where it's going, I can focus on building my top-line revenue and responsibly manage my bottom-line expenses without all the clutter of ambiguity getting in the way.

Set a weekly meeting with yourself or your family to review finances. Before you start the weekly financial review, go from funk to fantastic using one of the earlier strategies we discussed to be sure you are approaching your financial situation from a dynamic, optimistic perspective. Following that meeting, park your emotional heaviness about money until your next weekly financial review.

Digging yourself out of a financial hole is a long-term effort, so thinking about it every minute of every day doesn't help solve the problem. All the wallowing in the world won't move your bank account into the black. Rather than spend time worrying, start solving your money woes.

Once you've established personal parameters around when you can engage in self-pity and worry, you need to shift your attention away from the pile of debt and mounting bill payments to solutions. There are always solutions.

I remember I was feeling especially defeated financially. Cash flow was strapped, bills were piling up and I just couldn't see how I was going to eliminate debt and be financially free. I'd been misled by a big company (for the second time) and cleared my schedule for six months to roll out a training program nationally. As part of the deal they ordered several thousand books. Naïve to business at the time, I didn't know the importance of getting terms in writing before counting on a sale nor did I understand that those kinds of deals are only negotiated with the person who authorizes the cheques. When my main contact left the company, I really had no recourse. With an inventory of books that I had to cover and months of a clear schedule looming in front of me, I knew I didn't have the money to invest to gain new momentum for my business. Fight, flight or freeze. I froze. I did nothing except try to ignore it. There came a point when I had no choice but to get back into high gear. I took a deep breath and dove into solution-finding mode.

I bought into the philosophy that you need money to make money. My assumption was that I needed a lot of resources to get new clients, I was wrong.

Here's how I changed my state from defeatist to optimistic and I hope you'll do the same thing.

I wrote an exhaustive list of absolutely everything that needed to happen to get new clients and gain cash flow momentum, everything from making a prospect list to creating a one-sheet promotional PDF to doing sales calls.

Then I reviewed the list and put a dollar sign beside anything that required a financial outlay. The truth was, less than 20 percent of the tasks that needed to happen to get the business on track cost money. What I needed was focused sweat equity and fewer excuses. There must have been at least 40 actions I could take on that list.

Instead of letting financial limitations hold me back any longer, I tackled the easiest, most important tasks first. By the time, I got to a point where I needed to spend money I already had new clients and thus cash flow rolling through the door, so I could invest in the pieces that required money.

A large part of succeeding financially has to do with what you believe you deserve. Even if you don't like being broke, it may be serving you in some twisted way. Being strapped financially is a good excuse to protect yourself from the fear of reaching your full potential.

I remember when I was finally completely out of debt and had some extra moola in the bank. My brother said, "Okay, here's your chance. What do you want to do? You have no constraints. You can live anywhere and do anything. What does that look like? Go do it, no excuses."

The thought of making a decision without any anchors terrified me at first. There was a comfort that came from having financial restrictions keeping me stuck in my comfort zone. It meant I had a valid excuse to stay small. Fear of not being good enough lingered underneath my confident exterior and I finally had to muster the courage to create a life out from under the cloud.

Ironically, my choice wasn't to change too much. You know you're happy when you have the freedom to choose something different and you stay where you are.

The point is, money is fluid. It comes, it goes. It's up to you to decide not to let financial ups and downs control your mood. Live expecting abundance and have faith that financially everything will work out, then take appropriate steps to earn more. Wishful thinking isn't the answer. Action is.

To dig out of a financial hole, you only have three options: find a practical way to make more money, trade services or cut expenses.

Even if you're stuck in a job that doesn't pay enough, you can find a way to make more money. For example, propose a commission bonus for doing extra work, apply for a promotion or start a business on the side. The gig economy gives you another resource to earn money.

You can do the exercise in Chapter 34: *Expect Miracles, Strategize Solutions* with financial constraints. Here are some quick ideas on how this may look.

- <u>Can't stop obsessing about debt:</u> As already suggested, set a weekly financial review appointment to analyze your situation. Review your revenue and expenses. Commit to putting all your financial stress into that time block freeing you to stop worrying throughout the week. Identify the good choices you made recently and where you could do better next week.

- <u>Can't build a new website to launch your e-commerce business:</u> Build it yourself using templates or find a co-op student who is talented and can do it well-enough to launch. Production, not perfection.

- <u>Can't buy a new piece of equipment to launch a new product line:</u> Start a Kickstarter campaign or approach the equipment manufacturer for an older, off-lease model to get you started or partner with someone who has the machine to use during their downtime until you can buy your own.

- <u>Can't pay the mortgage:</u> Get a roommate, post on Airbnb, consolidate your debt or refinance your mortgage (lower interest rates can help cash flow.)

- <u>Can't buy healthy vegetables and food:</u> Plant a vegetable garden and research inexpensive meal ideas.

Slowly, but surely, chip away at the debt and get yourself financially free. It may not happen in an instant, but consistent effort today will get you there eventually. When you do reach your financial goals, it will be worth the effort. In the meantime, no personal judgments or shame are required.

Resiliency Ninja Formula

Self-Awareness +

Strength (♡ Heart + Mental + Physical) +

Resourcefulness = Resiliency Ninja

 Money can have an emotional hold. Recognize your patterns and don't let your mood be determined by your bank account.

 Take steps to earn more money, trade services or reduce expenses, money can be within your control.

 If you're failing financially, ask yourself, "What do I believe I deserve?" Are you holding yourself back from abundance because you think you're not good enough?

52

Your Choice: Victim or Resiliency Ninja, Wallow or Hope

I RAN INTO A PROFESSIONAL colleague who has back pain and because of it walks with a cane. Since we had shared our pain stories with each other over the years, she was naturally curious as to how I have come to manage my pain so well without heavy medications and procedures like before.

My first answer was to reference this book. It's the culmination of all elements of the Resiliency Ninja formula that allows me to find strength even when bad things are happening.

My second answer was one powerful word: acceptance.

Stopping the daily internal me-against-adversity battle allowed me to make peace with my grumpy Smurf. Harmony, not resentment inspired a more joyful way of life.

The acceptance that it's a fact of life to have bad stuff flying at you allows you to flip your focus to decide how you'll handle adversity, obstacles and stressors that get in your way. Your ability to rise from your depths of hell and become even stronger is largely related to your desire to find hope rather than wallow in your negative circumstances.

In the short-term the easiest answer is to linger at a personal-pity-party and wish for things to magically improve. In the long-term, doing so will make you miserable.

Even if you've been living in the poor-me-mentality-rut for years, you have the power to become a master Resiliency Ninja. You can choose to be a victim or a victor. It starts with a decision to uncover the blessings in your current circumstances.

Acceptance doesn't mean you stop advocating for yourself; it means you find peace in today's reality.

As a Resiliency Ninja you'll learn to love the moment, both joys and sorrows, while striving for a better tomorrow, without judgment and self-doubt.

There are times when you will feel overwhelmed by the fog of adversity. The worst experiences can consume your line of sight and other senses making it nearly impossible to see the light at the end of the tunnel or feel its warmth.

I'm here to assure you that the light and warmth are there.

When you walk from a place of faith, believing, without a doubt, that you can be joyful, even during difficult times, then you'll keep training your Resiliency Ninja skills until you find the best path for you.

When challenges strike look to the Resiliency Ninja formula:

Self-awareness + Strength (Heart + Mental + Physical) + Resourcefulness = Resiliency Ninja.

What aspects of the formula need your attention first? What do you need so you'll be stronger and get through your bad situation? If you feel stuck, look up from the quicksand and find the lifelines being tossed to you – I guarantee you they are there. If you allow yourself to savor the blessings, they will be there for you to enjoy.

Mom and Winston C taught me that.

It is my hope that this book will inspire you to strike your best superhero pose in front of the proverbial fan, not because others expect you to, but because you know you can and you choose to be the superstar of your daily life.

I hope you will be more authentic in your struggles, resisting the urge to keep up with unrealistic appearances. And I hope that you will be more open to forgiving yourself and others, so you can break free from the anger and hurts.

Where you are today may not be where you expected to be by this point in your life. You may even wish that the difficulties you face are not on your path at all, but they are. So, embrace them. Use them to create a stronger you. Enjoy the journey to Resiliency Ninja. It's worth it.

About the Author

Hi! Welcome to *Married My Mom, Birthed a Dog: How to Be Resilient When Life Sucks!* After reading my book you already know more about me than most do, so I won't bore you with a typical formal bio.

My mission is to show you how to not let your stress, obstacles and adversities define your outcome. I know you have a story and even if the challenges feel like they won't stop flying at you, I want you to know you're not alone in your struggles. There is a way for you to succeed, no matter what you're experiencing.

As a keynote speaker at conferences, through my Resiliency Ninja with Allison Graham podcast, my videos, books, online training programs and as a business coach, I share my messages of resilience and give tools to achieve business success. Visit www.R-Ninja.com to explore the various ways to work with me and hire me to speak at your next event(s).

You may see me in the media too. I've had the privilege of sharing my messages through incredible outlets like the *Financial Post, Globe and Mail, Fast Company, Investment Executive, Huffington Post and The Bottom Line.* Each week, you can hear me on Global News AM980 for a segment called *Small Business Lessons from the Big Business Headlines.*

In 2006, I launched my business called Elevate Biz to teach people how to build profitable relationships and not just survive, but become a connected superstar, in business. The reality is that all the tactical ideas don't matter if you're not resilient and can't ride the ups and downs of life. That's why I wrote this book.

I hope you love it! Please tell me if you do and share this with a friend you believe needs this message.

Find me at the Resiliency Ninja website www.R-Ninja.com or on major social media outlets at @AllisonDGraham.